100 THINGS TO DO IN THE NEBRASKA SANDHILLS BEFORE YOU DIE

Stick horse barrel racing at the Logan County Fair in Stapleton.

100 THINGS TO DO IN THE NEBRASKA SANDHILLS BEFORE YOU DIE

ALAN J. BARTELS

REEDY PRESS

Reedy Press
PO Box 5131
St. Louis, MO 63139, USA
www.reedypress.com

Library of Congress Control Number: 2023938761

ISBN: 9781681064673

Design by Jill Halpin

Author photo by Jennifer Lewis
All other images by Alan J. Bartels

Printed in the United States of America
24 25 26 27   5 4

DEDICATION

This book is dedicated to my family for enduring my often-nomadic lifestyle and long hours and days away from home. It is also dedicated to the thousands of Nebraskans who have shared meals, a spare bed, bumpy off-road rides to remote locations, intimate family histories, and innate knowledge of their parts of Nebraska with me during my writing career. Far too many to mention here: I consider all of you my friends.

CONTENTS

Music and Entertainment

Sports and Recreation

Culture and History

Shopping and Fashion

PREFACE

The Nebraska Sandhills defies definition. Geologists disagree about how the region was formed. Figures tossed around by academics declare it 19,300, 21,000, or as large as 25,000 square miles in size. Maps depict the region of grass-covered sand dunes making up all or parts of 20, 25, and even 27 Nebraska counties.

For the purposes of this book, I am including events, attractions, and destinations from a 25-county contiguous chunk of the Sandhills. Included are important travel gems I've discovered near the periphery. And one more caveat: for the region itself I will use "Sandhills" and "sand hills" when referring to the rolling geologic formations that the region is named for. Readers will also see "Sandhillers" used in respectful reference to Sandhills residents. Some might say it's not a word. Well, it is now.

Pull over to take a photo and a local is likely to stop and ask, "Are you OK?" Show up at a county fair and the next thing you know you're tied to a cowboy for the three-legged race, or eating pie next to a tiny ranch woman with no qualms about diving armpit-deep to pull a stuck calf. She could likely drink you under the picnic table you're sitting on, too.

These people work hard. Their love—limitless. At first, they may politely keep newcomers at arm's length. Once you've earned their trust, you've gained a friendship that can persist through generations.

There is no place like it. If you find yourself in the Nebraska Sandhills, you've found natural beauty, adventure, salt-of-the-earth people, clean air, and the best-tasting water on the planet. Drink it in. The Sandhills await, and your adventure begins now.

Bob Nichols, keeper of Mignery Sculpture Garden in Bartlett.

ACKNOWLEDGMENTS

Thank you to everyone at Reedy Press for your guidance, creativity, and for developing this entertaining book concept. I would also like to thank my many friends in the world of newspaper, magazine, and book publishing who have given my words, thoughts, and photos precious space over the bulk of the past two decades.

Thanks also to John Murphy, WBA, who through his spotting scope, gentle demeanor, and appreciation for both the simple and fine things in life, showed me how to take joy in observing nature without disturbing it; and to Bruce Switzer, his wife, Sue Ann, and their kin, who taught me the importance of family and place.

The idea for this book was born over brews at Kinkaider Brewing Company (KBC) in Broken Bow. Many thanks to the KBC crew past and present, including Cody, Nate, Barry, Dan, Alice, Jesse, Aubrey, Belinda, Megan, and LB.

The events, attractions, and services included in this book are of my own choosing and are not meant to be an all-inclusive account of what there is to see, do, or experience in the Nebraska Sandhills. This book will help you discover your own favorites. Additional travel information can be found through the Nebraska Tourism Commission, visitnebraska.com; Nebraska Traveler, nebraskatravelerguide.com; *Nebraska Life* magazine, nebraskalife.com; and the Western Nebraska Tourism Coalition, westnebraska.com.

The Sandhills Philly
at Kinkaider Brewing Company in Broken Bow.

FOOD AND DRINK

1

STRIKE SANDHILLS GOLD
AT SCRATCHTOWN BREWING COMPANY

"Call it Scratchtown," was Gen. Edward Ord's quick quip when Valley County residents suggested naming their new town after him. It was the early 1870s. Ord's unit was surveying the North Loup River Valley, and swarms of stinging, biting insects had the men scratching themselves raw.

Modern-day explorers scratch their itch for flavorful craft beers at Scratchtown Brewing Company. The general's quote appears on one wall, and the bloodsuckers inspiring Scratchtown's name hover in its logo. Most maps don't show this community of 2,100 residents as being in the Sandhills. But with Ord having a viable claim as the eastern gateway to the region, Scratchtown's owners bill their brews as the "Sandhills' Finest." Scratchtown's beer names ooze community and culture. For example, there's Sandhills Gold Blonde Ale, Popcorn Daze Cream Ale (Valley County is home to the world's most productive popcorn farmers), and Scarlet and Cream Amber Ale (named for the Nebraska Cornhuskers football team—Go, Big Red!). At Scratchtown, being a Sandhiller is a state of mind. We'll drink to that.

141 S 16th St., Ord, 308-728-5050, scratchtown.beer

TIP

With local brews, food trucks, games, live polka music, and dancing, Scratchtoberfest at Scratchtown Brewing Company each September is a celebration of harvest, heritage, and community pride.

DOUGH YOURSELF A FLAVORFUL FAVOR
AT PIZZA PALACE

Beer and pizza are a classic combination, but the pies at Pizza Palace stand on their own. When Calamus Reservoir (#45) was being built near Burwell in the early 1980s, the workmen overflowed the town's eateries at mealtime. Nary a seat was left for locals. Two Burwell teachers polled their students: What type of restaurant did the town need? The student body voted for a pizza place, and Pizza Palace soon was born.

Andrea Seidel worked at Pizza Palace during high school. She later bought the business. Her Calamus Reuben Pizza honors the lake so important to the region's economy, and the iconic Reuben sandwich invented 200 miles away in Omaha. A favorite of visitors—with mayo, ketchup, sweet pickle relish, and sauerkraut—this pizza has a tangy twang. Locals like their kraut, too. The popular Max Wilson Special is named for the Burwell man who always orders sauerkraut and hamburger on his pizza. This Sandhills pizzeria is upper-crust.

204 Grand Ave., Burwell, 308-346-5200, facebook.com/pizzapalaceinburwell

TIP

The Garfield County Historical Museum displays what is believed to be the saddle of notorious horse thief Doc Middleton. Before you leave Burwell, check out the rare railroad turntable on the west side of town on H St., the end of the line long ago.

308-346-4786

3

DIVE INTO NEBRASKA'S BEST REUBEN

AT THE DOUBLE T BAR

Lots of dive bars hang vintage beer lights, antlers, and even electronic, singing fish. When it comes to eclectic barroom décor, Double T Bar owner Reta Teahon says, "Hold my beer!" Her collection of quirk—including rattlesnake skins, a gas-powered airplane, and a mannequin's legs dangling through the ceiling—accumulated during more than half a century in business. For the 68 residents of Halsey, the establishment that Lee and Reta Teahon started in 1972 serves as the village's only bar and restaurant. Cowboy coffee boils every morning.

A Sandhills cowboy himself, the late Lee Teahon had a coolness factor matched only by the mythical Marlboro Man. He was an equal opportunity prankster. With a sly smile, Teahon would good-heartedly pick on everyone, whether he knew them or not. A painting of the legend overlooks diners enjoying chicken, steak, or the Double T Reuben—Nebraska's best, in my opinion—because it's made with three slices of bread and served with a side of Sandhills ambiance found nowhere else.

103 Main St., Halsey, 308-533-2208

HALSEY AREA SERVICES

Redwood Inn
503 NE Hwy. 2, Halsey, 308-533-2240
redwoodinnhalsey@gmail.com

Pine Street Cabin
804 N Pine St., Halsey, 308-880-1212
pinestreetcabin@gmail.com

Middle Loup River Ranch Guest House
40203 NE Hwy. 2, Thedford, 402-430-6794
info@middleloupriverranch.com

Sandhill Sutton's Speed & Supply
(groceries, hair salon, ATV supplies)
604 NE Hwy. 2, Halsey, 308-533-2323

The Spur
(fuel, convenience store, bar/grill)
Intersection of Hwys. 2 and 91, Dunning, 308-538-2251

Norm's Auto Repair
Intersection of Hwys. 2 and 91, Dunning, 308-538-2263

Sandhill Oil Company
(fuel, convenience store, tire repair, liquor, Western art)
39397 NE Hwy. 2, Thedford, 308-645-2233
sandhilloil.com

Roadside Inn
39357 NE Hwy. 2, Thedford, 308-645-2284
roadsideinn.net

Anthem Coffee
39295 NE Hwy. 2. Thedford, 308-645-2381
facebook.com/anthemcoffeeco

4

PIG OUT
AT THE HUNGRY HORSE SALOON

Downtown Ericson looks like it's right out of 1886, the year the B&O Railroad platted the community. Central Avenue, Ericson's main drag, was built wide for horses and wagons. Nowadays, people park down the center of the gravel street while chowing down at Hungry Horse Saloon.

Hungry Horse is open 365 days a year, often tripling its population of 89 on Friday, Saturday, and Sunday nights while serving scrumptious prime rib. Big eaters order the 18-ounce King. Diners with smaller appetites go for the equally tasty 12-ounce Queen. While prime rib royalty is served weekends only, this menu features beef all week long. When I first walked into the Hungry Horse in the early 1980s, a livestock tank with a herd of turtles inside was sitting on the dance floor. Ericson is no longer Nebraska's turtle racing capital, but travelers still race here for the food. If you're eating at the Hungry Horse, you won't ride away hungry.

520 Central Ave., Ericson, 308-653-2100, facebook.com/hungryhorsesaloon

TIP

Legend has it that a verbal agreement gone wrong when the Hungry Horse came up for sale years ago led to creation of the Starvin' Stallion Saloon. Today it's known as the Wagon Wheel Saloon & Steakhouse, where visitors stampede in for prime rib sandwiches, cheesy hashbrowns, and Thursday night steak and shrimp dinners.

823 NE Hwy. 91, Ericson, 308-653-3100

5

SET YOUR SIGHTS
ON OLE'S

No Sandhills safari is complete without dining with the local animals in Paxton. This isn't a jab at the community's 530 residents. What I'm roaring about is getting a bite at Ole's Big Game Steakhouse and Lounge. After pitcher Rosser O. Herstedt won a baseball game and the opposing team couldn't scrape up his $50 payment, they gave Herstedt (Ole) an ornate walnut bar. Ole put it in his parents' downtown Paxton building and opened for business at one minute after midnight when Prohibition ended in 1933.

Herstedt hung a whitetail deer head in his bar before keeping his taxidermist busy with exotic game harvested during hunting adventures around the world. Just inside the front door stands the polar bear that Herstedt shot on a Russian ice floe. An African elephant looks over the dining room. Smaller animals are displayed, too, including waterfowl from the nearby Platte River. The menu at Ole's features Nebraska beef, bison, and cold beer.

123 N Oak St., Paxton, 308-239-4500, olesbiggame.com

TIP

When Paxton's landmark grain elevator was destined for the scrapyard, resident Leah Fotes bought it, moved it, and turned it into a coffee shop. Now known as The Grainery, it sits next to the 1890s Union Pacific railroad depot where Fotes operates an antique store, adjacent to her 20-acre Aronia berry field.

thegraineryne.com

6

SHOOT STRAIGHT
INTO THE L BOW ROOM BAR

Johnstown's 63 residents agree: the L Bow Room Bar has the best food in town. Never mind that the bar and grill in a former bank is Johnstown's only dining establishment. The bar is made of local cedar wood. Cattle brands adorn the walls. A ragged bobcat mount lurks in a corner. A sign reads, "Never climb a barbed wire fence naked." That's good advice. Here's some more: The Sandhills may be Nebraska's Wild West, but don't come in here loaded or half-cocked.

Ruth Trobee, who owns the bar with her husband, Leonard (Bud), recalls when the local firemen met in the bar. One mentioned getting a new gun, and the others wanted to see it. He brought the firearm inside and began passing it around—until someone tripped the trigger. While serving patrons, the Trobees point out where the bullet whizzed by one man's head and through the wall. The L Bow Room Bar *aims* to please.

101 Main St., Johnstown, 402-722-4481

TIP

The Brown County Fair & Rodeo takes place at the Brown County Fairgrounds in Johnstown every Labor Day weekend.
nebraskafairs.org

7

PULL OVER
AT HWY 14 BREWING COMPANY

Highways 14, 39, and 91 meet in the Boone County community of Albion. Whether you arrive via plane, train, or automobile, every visit to Albion should include a pit stop at the HWY 14 Brewing Company. When owner Greg Luettel (pronounced Little) was looking to scale up his home-brewing hobby from his basement and garage to commercial production, he and his wife, Mandy, toured building after historical building before finding just the right one in a former floral shop in downtown Albion. It didn't hurt that the structure, built in 1919, already was equipped with a pair of working walk-in coolers. Exposed brick walls and ornate tin ceilings are reminiscent of Albion a century ago. The Smoyer-Wathen Monument is just down the street. HWY 14 named one of their beers after those fallen hometown crimefighters. Smoyer-Wathen's Revenge is a tasty, blood-orange IPA. HWY 14 has cans and glass growlers to go. Life is *brewtiful* in the Sandhills.

134 S 4th St., Albion, 402-395-8733, facebook.com/hwy14brewingco

TIP

McPherson County was Nebraska's last "dry" county, with no alcohol legally sold here from 1890, when the county was founded, to 2004. The $700 raised by auctioning the first legal beer benefitted an educational scholarship.

TOAST PATRIOTISM
AT BOLO BEER CO.

This Valentine brewery is all about taste, fun, and honoring where you come from. Canoes dented during Niobrara River floats are docked in the rafters. Bolo pays homage to ranching with Cattle Barron—an imperial stout. I always order an Americus India Pale Ale (IPA). The brewery's founders say it's "straightforward and approachable, like its namesake."

Americus Liberator came to the Sandhills after toiling in Pennsylvania coal mines and threw his cowboy hat into the US presidential race—five times! His platform was simple: he wanted Americans to see horses grazing on the White House lawn. Liberator made headlines traveling the campaign trail in 1968, wearing a white suit on the back of his white horse, Pard. The animal's likeness is etched into Liberator's headstone in Valentine. Liberator never became commander in chief, but he made history as the only candidate defeated by Ronald Reagan three times (1968, 1976, 1980). We raise a glass to this Sandhills notable. Bolo displays a Liberator campaign poster—and also brews Liberator—a double IPA. Cheers!

420 E 1st St., Valentine, 402-259-5180, bolobeer.com

MORE FLAVORS OF VALENTINE

Old Mill Bulk Food
A dine-in deli, bakery, grocery store, and pizza joint.
704 E C St., 402-376-8034
facebook.com/oldmillbulkfoodsvalentinene

The Peppermill & E. K. Valentine Lounge
Features a menu packed with beef, daily specials, creative desserts, cocktails, and a selection of craft beers.
502 E US Hwy. 20, 402-376-2800
peppermillvalentine.com

Bunkhouse Restaurant and Saloon
Homestyle cooking, steaks, and cocktails.
109 W US Hwy. 20, 402-376-1609
facebook.com/bunkhousene

Raine Restaurant and Lounge
Authentic Indian fare with an attached hotel. Open seasonally.
618 W US Hwy. 20, 402-389-2322
rainerestaurantlounge.com

Janine's Flower Exchange
A flower shop and espresso bar.
262 N Main St., 402-376-2257
janinesflower.com

Somethin' Else Cafe
Serves breakfast and lunch.
733 US Hwy. 20, 402-376-9261

Sandhills Art & Metal Gallery
It may seem out of place in this dining directory if not for the homemade ice cream whipped up alongside stunning artwork.
265 N Main St., 402-376-1839
sandhillsartandmetalgallery.com

9

CHOW DOWN
AT D&B CAFE IN AINSWORTH

Introduced to me by a friend years ago, this small-town cafe provided a gigantic omelet and mound of hashbrowns on my first visit. Owner Connie Kelly goes through 250 pounds of spuds each week. She had $750 left in her pocket after buying the café in 2002, but locals, visitors, and hardworking family staff members, along with her homestyle cooking, have made it a success.

You can't go wrong with a D&B Burger. They are hand-patted, the fries are hand-cut, and the ranch sauce is homemade. My eyes were bigger than my stomach last time and I ordered one of Kelly's cinnamon rolls. She makes them according to her Aunt Jen's secret recipe. A batch takes six hours to make, and each roll tips the scale at over a pound. The letters D and B stand for previous owners Dick and Betty, but in the case of these rolls and the burgers, they stand for delicious and big!

202 N Richardson Dr., Ainsworth, 402-387-9902

TIP

Interpretive signage 6 miles south of Ainsworth on Nebraska Hwy. 7 explains the technology of the 36 wind turbines at the Ainsworth Wind Energy Facility.

10

LICK YOUR CHOPS
AT BULLDOGGER'S BBQ

If there's anything more American than a small-town barbecue joint, it's Bulldogger's BBQ in downtown Valentine. Heath Bristol, who owns Bulldogger's with his wife, Courtney, served in the US Navy. The couple gives a discount to military veterans. As a veteran myself, I salute the Bristols for their generosity.

Customers sit at picnic tables outside or take orders to-go. The menu includes brisket, pulled pork, chicken, spareribs, and smoked sausage. All the meat is smoked in-house. The sauces—spicy, sweet, and Carolina—are homemade, too, as are the coleslaw, potato salad, branding beans, and the other side dishes. Heath is a Valentine native. Courtney is from the southern US, which explains the southern sweet tea on the menu. The Bristols told me that this veteran- and woman-owned business is the only barbecue joint for more than 100 miles. Bulldogger's is seasonal, open April through October, and sometimes earlier or later, depending on the weather.

223 S Main St., Valentine, 402-376-2786, facebook.com/bulldoggersbbq

TIP

The Coachlight Cafe's Peanut Butter Bacon Badger Burger weighs in at a full pound, while inspiring community pride. There's no badger meat on this big boy—the name refers to Valentine's school mascot. Go, Badgers!
302 N Main St., 402-376-3145

WINE A LITTLE
AT NIOBRARA VALLEY VINEYARDS

The Sandhills isn't considered "wine country." When "experts" told brothers Tim and Greg Nollette that wine grapes wouldn't grow in the Sandhills, these two high school agriculture teachers tried, anyway. Twenty years later, the Nollette family makes and sells award-winning wines from their cattle ranch south of Nenzel. "This is cow country and I'm a rancher. When it was time for a drink, I'd drink beer or whiskey," Greg Nollette told me. "It's not considered manly to belly up to the bar and order a glass of chardonnay, but that's changing."

Wine names like Boss Cow, Homesteader, and Blackberry Blizzard pay homage to Sandhills ranching culture. The tasting room bar top is made of cedar from the ranch. This island of grapes within an ocean of grass is closed Monday and Tuesday, May through September. It's open by appointment the rest of the year. Pizzas bake on Friday nights, and make sure to ask about their fourth Sunday prime rib dinners. After all, like Greg says, this is cow country.

90256 State Spur 16F, Nenzel, 402-823-4131, nvvsandhills.net

TIP

From Nenzel, travel south on NE Spur 16-F for 18 miles to reach Samuel R. McKelvie National Forest.

fs.usda.gov

12

LIVE LARGE
AT BIG JOHN'S RESTAURANT

If you're arriving at Ainsworth on US Highway 20, one feature dominates the community's skyline—Big John. The giant sign, depicting a muscular young lad with one hand on his hip and the other balancing a tray topped with a burger and soft drink, has been an Ainsworth landmark for decades. Owner John Stec started the business in 1980. As far as he knows, his Big John sign is the only one in existence. Last time I was there he said the sign is 20 to 30 feet tall, and that his own boyhood nickname was "Big John."

Big John's offers nightly specials, a Sunday lunch buffet, and plenty of homestyle cooking. The Big John Burger and homemade dinners are the most popular items on the menu. I usually order the Big John Steak Sandwich and the salad bar. The pork tenderloin sandwich is a whopping thing of beauty.

1110 E 4th St., Ainsworth, 402-387-0500, facebook.com/bigjohnsrestaurant

TIP

In most places, referring to a location as in the "middle of nowhere" is considered an insult. The expression is a point of pride in Ainsworth, where each June, the community celebrates its remoteness with carnival rides, food vendors, and more during the Middle of Nowhere Carnival Days celebration.

ainsworthchamber.com

13

SIP FLAVORS OF HAWAII
AT MARK FERRARI SPECIALTY COFFEES

Mark Ferrari came to Oshkosh from his family's macadamia nut and coffee farm in Kona, Hawaii. Ferrari liked the quiet community and welcoming residents of his business partner Mike Piva's hometown, and soon moved his Italian coffee roaster into a former downtown farm implement dealership.

Turns out that Oshkosh is a good central location for shipping coffee nationwide. Mark Ferrari Specialty Coffees didn't need to open a small coffee shop in the front of the building, but the community needed it. Ferrari's coffees have been described as "nutty, with a wine-like profile and chocolate-like aroma that captivates people's senses." His rare Kona coffee beans are grown only on the fertile slopes of Hawaii's Hualālai volcano. I suggest taking the tour, stocking up on bags of Kona Gold, and heading out the door with a steaming cup of Kona goodness toward your own Sandhills voyage.

209 W 1st St., Oshkosh, 308-772-0138, markferraricoffee.com

TIP

The many colorful murals in Oshkosh are the creative works of local art teacher Lauren Olson. So far, Olson has painted nearly 50 public works in the community, and in nearby Lewellen, Lisco, Chappell, Bridgeport, and Big Springs.

laurenolsonart.com

SAMPLE SUDS
AT THE WESTERN NEBRASKA CRAFT BEER FESTIVAL

The cooler temperatures of September are reason enough to celebrate with a cold one. Get an 18-pack or more of Nebraska craft breweries together on the edge of the Sandhills and the celebratory mood overflows. The Western Nebraska Craft Beer Festival takes place in the two-acre outdoor beer garden at Pals Brewing Company in North Platte. Cornhole and other games entertain as patrons line up for a cornucopia of brews.

Pals's famous pizza is served by the slice outside at the Grain Bin Bar. The brewery opened in 2017 and founded the festival a year later so beer patrons could sample suds from across Nebraska. Beer fans taking advantage of the festival's VIP option get one-on-one time with brewery owners and the brewers. Pals is open year-round with 17 beers on tap, pizzas, and other favorites, with lodging available at Pals's Bed & Brew, just down the street.

4520 S Buffalo Bill Ave., North Platte, 308-221-6715, palsbrewingcompany.com

TIP

A rustic boardwalk connects 20 historic, octagonal granaries south of North Platte at Grain Bin Antique Town. Each one overflows with bushels of antiques, collectibles, primitives, and other must-have items.
facebook.com/grainbinantiquetown, 308-539-7401

15

GET A KICK

OUT OF PEG LEG BREWING COMPANY

North Platte has another brewery. Peg Leg Brewing Company attracts attention with its unique name, but it's no gimmick. Head brewer Mike Sullivan, aka "Captain Pegleg," has worn a prosthetic leg since learning to walk. Peg Leg is home to the "peg-o-lier," a wagon-wheel chandelier hanging above the bar and adorned with nine of Sullivan's prosthetic legs—even the small ones from his youth. "Not too creepy," he told me. This brewery within sight of Interstate 80 gets creative with its beer names. You gotta love their "Bock to the Future." I know I do. That beer goes great with their pub munchies. Four hotels within walking distance makes Peg Leg a great place for beer lovers to sample a flight and then stay the night.

Peg Leg Brewing Company may not have a leg up over other breweries, but hands down, they're making beer here that some brewers would give an arm AND a leg for—figuratively speaking, of course.

2519 Halligan Dr., North Platte, 308-252-1658

TIP

The North Platte Canteen, where volunteers from 125 communities met troop trains during World War II, is no longer standing. Lincoln County Museum explains its impact through exhibits. In North Platte's Historic Canteen District, The Cedar Room was named "Best Steakhouse in the US" by travel magazine *Travel Awaits*.

visitnorthplatte.com

SAVOR FLAVOR
IN CODY

Necessity inspired Sandhills pioneers to build with sod or hay. Those old ways persist in Cody. From a straw bale building on Nebraska Avenue, George Johnson makes vinegar. The two-foot-thick bale walls hold warmth in winter and provide cool relief during summer. Making his product gentle and slow imparts flavorful complexities like old-world vinegars and unlike most mass-produced varieties. Johnson proves it with vinegar tastings for visitors—including vanilla ice cream drizzled with his raspberry vinegar.

The aged vinegars created by Johnson and his daughter, Emily, at George Paul Vinegar are shipped to New York City, Los Angeles, Denver, Omaha, and upscale restaurants in between. Visitors can also find them at Circle C Market, the grocery store in Cody that is operated by students from Cody-Kilgore Unified Schools. The store also is built out of bales.

302 E Nebraska Ave., Cody, 402-823-4067, georgepaulvinegar.com

TIP

In addition to necessities for area ranchers, the inventory at Cody Livestock Supply includes candles, footwear, jewelry, home décor, gift items, toys, and books. Kids love the store cat, Lucy.

109 W US Hwy. 20, 402-823-4241

OTHER CHERRY COUNTY DESTINATIONS

From his **Sandhills Boot Company** in Cody, Kyle Rosfeld crafts cowboy boots using century-old methods. He fitted actress Daryl Hannah for boots, and country singer Willie Nelson and rocker Neil Young each own a pair.
102 N Walnut St., Cody, 402-376-5960
madeintheneb.com

As the grouse flies, Kilgore is less than 5 miles from the Nebraska–South Dakota border. The appropriately named **Bordertown Steakhouse & Saloon** is on Main St. in Kilgore and known for its Tap Tuesday, Wing Wednesday, and Sunday prime rib specials.
100 Main St., Kilgore, 402-966-3881
facebook.com/bordertownsteakhouse

From the unincorporated community of Crookston, scenic Sandhills drives begin on **German Settlement Road**. Please tread lightly, and don't you dare trespass.

Cherry County is also home to **Fort Niobrara National Wildlife Refuge**. At more than 19,000 acres, it offers spacious views of the Niobrara River Valley, as well as elk, bison, deer, and other wildlife.
39983 Refuge Rd., Valentine

BELLY UP TO THE BAR
AT KINKAIDER BREWING COMPANY (KBC)

I'm a sucker for anything with "Sandhills" in the name. At this farm brewery/restaurant, the Sandhills Philly sandwich oozes with provolone cheese and earthy green peppers. There's another peppery offering here drawing travelers and craft beer fans.

KBC cofounder Dan Hodges, "Dan the Wiser," spent 10 years perfecting Devil's Gap Jalapeno Ale. The beer is named for the canyon where the Olive Gang hanged and then burned two homesteaders in 1878. "Thus ended the last act of drama of blood . . . unequaled in the annals of crime in the great west," said Broken Bow photographer Solomon Butcher. Kinkaider's "Frame the Butcher" is an India Pale Ale named for the photographer who framed up homesteaders and Kinkaid Act settlers posed with their sod homes. Historical images from the era adorn the brewery. In addition to beer and cider on 18 taps, Kinkaider offers on-site lodging with a beer fridge in the shower.

43860 Paulsen Rd., Broken Bow, 308-872-8348, kinkaiderbrewing.com

TIP

Pioneer photographer Solomon Butcher's images are displayed at the Custer County Museum, along with the last remaining fragment of the splintered Pawnee bow that the community of Broken Bow is named for.

445 S 9th Ave., Broken Bow, 308-872-2203

MORE SANDHILLS DINING OPTIONS

Bibs and Boots Cafe
Chicken Fried Steak
1 Randolph St., Bartlett, 308-654-3335

Antelope Creek Cafe
Sandhills Scrambler
107 E US Hwy. 20, Gordon, 308-282-2754

Sandhills Corral
Rocky Mountain Oysters
39359 NE Hwy. 2, Thedford, 308-645-2323

Ken and Dales Restaurant
B-B-B-B-BLT sandwich (with 5 strips of bacon)
123 E 3rd St., Alliance, 308-762-7252

Lazy D Restaurant & Lounge
Pan-Fried Chicken
308 3rd St., Taylor, 308-942-3400

The Chubby Rhino Tavern
Baby Rhino Burger
315 Main St., Oshkosh, 308-772-1011

Playing in the shade at Carson Ranch.

MUSIC AND ENTERTAINMENT

18

SNAG PARADE CANDY
AT NEBRASKALAND DAYS

This "Official State Celebration of Nebraska" has been a North Platte tradition since 1968. It's a fitting location for a celebration right out of the Wild West—William F. "Buffalo Bill" Cody was living in North Platte when he came up with the idea for America's first spectator rodeo. A convincing Cody lookalike, atop his trusty steed, leads the NEBRASKAland Days Parade. Visitors line up along East Fourth and Dewey Streets in anticipation. My favorite spot is in the Lincoln County Courthouse lawn. Last time I was there, I approached a rancher sitting under a tree and asked how much he was charging for shade. His wife chimed in with, "How much you got?"

The Wild West Arena where many NEBRASKAland Days events take place is right across the street from Buffalo Bill Ranch State Historical Park. The June celebration includes the Buffalo Bill Rodeo, an art show, carnival, beer garden, games, a car show, and concerts. The real Buffalo Bill would be proud.

2801 Charlie Evans Dr., North Platte, 308-532-7939, nebraskalanddays.com

TIP

The Prairie Arts Center is housed in North Platte's historic 1913 Federal Building. In addition to the main gallery, there's a reception room and a catering kitchen, workshop space, private art studios, and the Wildflower Gift Shop.

416 N Jeffers St., North Platte, 308-534-5121

WIN A CAKE
AT THE LOUP COUNTY WORLD'S FAIR

Calling this celebration the "Loup County World's Fair" might seem like hyperbole to outsiders. But to Loup County residents, this four-day extravaganza in Taylor means the world. Ribbons are won during livestock shows and open-class competitions. The craft fair takes place in the community center, and the free-will donation hamburger and hot dog feed is in Taylor Park. High schoolers from Loup County Public Schools serve visitors during the Pork and Beef Feed.

Like any respectable county fair, there's a car show, parade, beer garden, and a dance. Barrel racing, roping, and a junior rodeo are also on the schedule. Orchestrating the celebration is no cakewalk—it takes a village—and the cakewalk is one of the most popular events. For only 25 cents per try, you could win a cake baked using a longtime ranching family's secret recipe. That'll bring people out of the hills. After all, this is the Sandhills—a world of its own.

The Loup County World's Fair takes place on the town square in Taylor.
loupcountyworldsfair.org

TIP

A group of Taylor promoters is working to increase tourism while honoring the memory of a teacher who loved the community. When completed, the Kevin Brown Educators Memorial Trail will leave Taylor, cross the North Loup River, and stretch into surrounding hills.
facebook.com/kbemt

CLAP TO OLD COUNTRY
AT CARSON RANCH

Sandhillers work hard. When fences are fixed, hay baled, and the cattle moo-ved, Carson Ranch celebrates with a musical shindig in Goose Creek Valley. Spectators bring a side dish for the potluck dinner or drop a donation into the cream can. Ranch owners Dan and Shirley Carson supply the meat. There are hamburgers on Friday night, bacon and eggs the next morning, and brisket for supper on Saturday.

The Carson Ranch Annual Music Jam and Festival began in the early 2000s. While some performers play in the Carson Concert Hall (it's a workshop most of the year), others spread out in the shady lawn for acoustic sets among friends old and new. The ranch is on Dobro Lane. The dobro is one of Dan's favorite instruments. He can also strum tunes on the guitar and mandolin. In addition to Shirley, Dan's loves are cattle and old country music. The Carsons happily host music lovers at their Sandhills ranch during the first weekend in July.

84811 Dobro Ln., Purdum, 308-834-3284

TIP

Harsh Mercantile is one of the oldest continually operating businesses in Nebraska. Locally owned since 1899, it sells hardware, groceries, hot coffee, and more necessities.

84453 Purdum Ave., Purdum, 308-834-3251

21

SCOOT YOUR BOOTS
AT THE NORDEN BARN DANCE

In the early days of Sandhills settlement, ranch families helped one another with brandings and other chores. Afterward, they danced the night away in the barn loft. Neighbors still help each other, but barn dances are mostly a thing of the past. But not in unincorporated Norden. The Norden Dance Hall has been a celebratory staple since this barn-like structure's first dance in 1932. The biweekly summer through fall Saturday night dances regularly draw 400 to 600 boot-scooters, electric sliders, and tush-pushers. The crowd swells to 1,200 two-steppers during the Keya Paha County Fair in August.

In addition to the regular dance, there were six birthdays and a wedding celebration taking place during my first visit. The oak dance floor was elbow to elbow; the temperature,16 degrees. There hadn't been a colder dance here since 1941. Although my two left feet were frozen, this barn is piled high with bales of warm and welcoming community spirit.

29 miles east of Valentine on Nebraska Hwy. 12 near mile marker 29
402-497-3756

TIP

The Nature Conservancy's Niobrara Valley Preserve protects 56,000 acres near the Niobrara River, including the Norden Chute. Bison graze its sprawling grasslands. Includes public trails.
42269 Morel Rd., Johnstown, 402-722-4440

22

DANCE AN IRISH JIG
IN GREELEY

South of O'Neill (#60), Greeley challenges as Nebraska's true Irish Capital—and that's no blarney. Government statistics prove Greeley has the highest percentage of residents of Irish descent in Nebraska. Seeing no reason to celebrate their Irishness only once a year, they founded the Greeley Irish Festival.

I attended Greeley High School (Go, Bulldogs!). Greeley's Irish pride is apparent in streets named Galway, Kerry, and O'Connor. A sign reads, "Greeley: 562 friendly people and a few old crabs." The festival features an Irish Culture Center, cornhole tournament, and the Nebraska Cornhuskers football game in the Big Red Tent. Bands from the motherland entertain into the wee hours. I recommend lining up for Irish stew and soda bread from the local Catholic Daughters. The Beer Tent lines are even longer, but I know from experience that they move fast. Sláinte!

West of the intersection of W Burke Ave. and N Clare St., Greeley
308-428-5595, greeleyirishfestival.com

TIP

Whereas the Greeley Irish Festival is always the third Saturday in September, Greeley Days takes place the third weekend in July.
greeleyne.com

SING A TUNE
AT OLD WEST DAYS

Most Sandhills cowboys I know don't say much. When they do speak, it is thought-out and meaningful. The same can be said of the verse voiced at the Old West Days & Nebraska Cowboy Poetry Gathering in Valentine. Poets, musicians, and storytellers have gathered for this event for more than 30 years. That's a lot of alliteration, rhymes, and . . . pauses, for effect. Performers include local and nationally known entertainers.

The event at Valentine High School includes free poetry and music sessions, writing workshops, a trail ride, and my favorite—the Western Art, Trade, and Quilt Show. Leather tack, tanned animal skins, antler crafts, and flavorful concoctions in little glass jars are bestsellers here. Last time I was blown away by the creations of Valentine artists David Dorsey and Patricia Schemmer, and Valentine art teacher Joan Swim. I left with a copper wire sculpture by Ken Bennett that I cherish as a reminder of the Sandhills.

431 N Green St., Valentine, 833-693-7638, oldwestdays.net

TIP

Find out about Joan Swim's plein air painting workshops at her "Paint Along the Niobrara River" Facebook page.

THROW A POT
AT CALINDA'S POT SHOP & ART GALLERY

Artist Linda Lacy portrays the Sandhills on canvas and in clay. She displays that creativity in Ashby, an unincorporated community that Lacy told me has about 40 residents, "if you count cats and dogs." Her works reveal ranch scenes, windmills, and Sandhills flora and fauna. Though no medicinal herbs are available at the curiously named shop, Lacy does host a Kid's Summer Art Camp, pottery workshops, and Sip and Stroke painting events where patrons bring beverages of choice and learn to paint.

The gallery in a former cafe brings vibrance to Ashby's quiet Main Street. Vintage booths serve as display space, so Lacy's customers relax on the Party Porch with specialty coffees or smoothies as coal trains roar by. The Soapweed Squeeze, named for the yucca plants found nearby, is a culinary work of ice cream art served in an antique soda fountain glass.

113 Main St., Ashby, 308-458-8051, calindaspotshop.com

TIP

Ashby is in an area of natural lakes with creative names such as Bean Soup Lake, Soda Lake, Castle Lake, Coffee Lake, and Dipping Vat Lake. Most Sandhills lakes are on private property, so please do not trespass.

SMALL-TOWN STOPS

The University of Nebraska's **Gudmundsen Sandhills Laboratory** is a working ranch and research station.
45089 Gudmundsen Rd., Whitman, 308-544-6515

Congregants from **Bingham Lutheran Church** raised funds recently to restore the church's 8-foot-tall stained glass windows. Tours are available. Call first.
1084 McAdoo Ave., Bingham, 308-458-9685

25

SAFARI THROUGH NEBRASKA'S SERENGETI
AT STABLE PRODUCTIONS

Zebras grazing grassy savannahs are what many people envision when they think of Africa. This scene takes place in the Sandhills, too. Across the Middle Loup River from Seneca, zebras, water buffalo, elands, alpacas, aoudads, bison, camels, and other exotic critters graze in riverside meadows. There is even a tortoise, porcupines, emus, and a kangaroo!

The menagerie at Stable Productions spreads out across 600 acres between the river and a towering ridge of sand hills. Founder Flip Licking's mission is providing children, people with disabilities, and veterans with unforgettable experiences through interacting with exotic animals from around the world. As Christmas nears, he loads up his reindeer herd to spread holiday joy. Licking also takes his petting zoo on the road. Ranch tours and other activities are available, and so are overnight stays in Licking's barn. Please call before visiting.

37950 Avey Ln., Seneca, 308-650-0162, stableproranch.org

TIP

Even though sand hills are the only peaks for miles, heading west out of Seneca takes travelers into the Mountain time zone.

AIM FOR HISTORY
AT CRYSTAL PALACE REVUE

Ogallala was so violent in the 1870s that it became known as the "Gomorrah of the Plains." The trouble came from Texas Trail cowboys looking for fun after months on the cattle trail. The community has cleaned up its act, but shots still ring out on Front Street. That's the part of Ogallala built six decades ago to resemble a Wild West town.

During the Crystal Palace Revue's summer season, teenage actors perform as cowboys, outlaws, lawmen, and saloon girls. The show begins outside with a gunfight. The rounds are blanks, in what is the oldest summer stock theater in Nebraska. The actors and crowd step over the "victims" and into the Crystal Palace Saloon for supper and the show depicting the history of the Old West, Ogallala, and Nebraska with hilarity and fun. Front Street includes a general store and free museum.

519 E 1st St., Ogallala, 308-284-6000, ogallalafrontstreet.com

TIP

Across US Hwy. 30 from Front St., the Petrified Wood Gallery displays the ancient finds and artwork of twin brothers Harvey and Howard Kenfield, as well as Native American artifacts and the art of other artists. 418 E 1st St., Ogallala, 308-284-9996

MORE OGALLALA-AREA ATTRACTIONS

Mansion on the Hill Museum preserves what was Ogallala's most opulent dwelling in the late 1880s.
1004 N Spruce St., Ogallala, 800-658-4390

Central Nebraska Public Power and Irrigation District operates a heated eagle viewing facility at Lake Ogallala in January and February. A Nebraska Park Entry Permit is required.
308-284-2332

Boot Hill Cemetery is the final resting place of cowboys, drifters, American Indians, gamblers, and peaceful citizens who perished at Ogallala in the 1870s and 1880s. A recreated wooden marker shows where Rattlesnake Ed was buried after being shot over a $9 bet.
10th St. and Parkhill Dr., Ogallala

Spruce Street Visitor Center is a restored 1922 Standard Oil filling station.
220 N Spruce St., Ogallala
308-284-0811

Prairie Theatre was built in 1936. It shows Hollywood movies, but the best show just might be the friendly spirits reported to inhabit the place.
208 N Spruce St., Ogallala, 308-284-4033

Tri-Trails Park is the meeting place of the historic Oregon Trail, Pony Express Trail, and the Great Western Cattle Trail.
Rd. W 80 and Lawrence Rd. Ogallala

Driftwood is a rustic restaurant in downtown Ogallala known for Lake Mac and Cheese, Morning Glory Walleye, the Johnny Carson Late Night Burger, live music, and cold beer.
118 N Spruce St., Ogallala, 308-284-7053
driftwoodogallala.com

Little Church of Keystone is a unique symbol of pioneer cooperation. In 1908, Keystone's residents built a church with a Protestant altar at one end and a Catholic altar at the other. Pews with reversible backs make it work.
Keystone Lake Rd. and McCarthy St., Keystone

Crusty's Feed Store carries an amazing variety of apparel, coolers, tack items, roping dummies, and one-of-a-kind Crusty's caps.
10 Swanson Dr., Arthur, 308-764-2259
crustysfeed.com

27

TRAIN YOUR EYES ON CHOO-CHOOS
AT GOLDEN SPIKE TOWER

There's something cool about trains snaking through the Sandhills. Twice, while I photographed trains from the roadside, law enforcement has stopped to check on me (both times in Hooker County). True train buffs get amazing views from atop North Platte's Golden Spike Tower.

The attraction overlooks Union Pacific's Bailey Yard, the largest railroad classification yard on earth. It handles 14,000 railcars on 315 miles of rail every day. Golden Spike Tower visitors watch the coming and going from the seventh-floor, open-air viewing deck, or the enclosed, eighth-floor viewing area. Exhibits explain the history of railroading. The gift shop is stocked with train collectibles, and a model choo-choo on tracks near the ceiling chugs around the room. Visitors explore real railcars outside.

1249 N Homestead Rd., North Platte, 308-532-9920, goldenspiketower.com

TIP

William F. "Buffalo Bill" Cody proudly called North Platte home. His Victorian house and 25 acres of his Scouts Rest Ranch remains for visitors to enjoy as Buffalo Bill Ranch State Historical Park.

2921 Scouts Rest Ranch Rd., North Platte, 308-535-8035

28

EXPLORE NATURE'S CLASSROOM
AT OLSON NATURE PRESERVE

A small finger of the Sandhills reaches into Boone County, where it meets loess hills, a cottonwood grove, oak forest, lowland tallgrass prairie, an oxbow wetland, and a sandy canyon. Beaver Creek flows for a half-mile through the important natural area known as Olson Nature Preserve (ONP). The preserve is named for farmers Grant and Bernice Olson. They had no children, but allowed scout groups and others to enjoy their land. Because of the Olson family's generosity, this 112-acre natural wonderland belongs to the Prairie Plains Resource Institute and is open to the public.

A trail winds through the property, beginning with a footbridge over the creek. Teachers from Boone Central High School in Albion use ONP as an outdoor classroom. It once was a destination for Native American bison hunts, and Omaha Chief Logan Fontenelle was killed in this area by a Sioux war party in 1855. Today, Olson Nature Preserve is a peaceful oasis on the edge of the Sandhills.

8 miles north of Albion on Nebraska Hwy. 14, then 1 mile west on Y Rd.
402-694-5535, prairieplains.org

TIP

A Nebraska Historical Marker dedicated to Logan Fontenelle stands along Front St. in Petersburg.

PARK IT
AT CARHENGE

The Sandhills has a quirky side. So did artist Jim Reinders. He became inspired by Stonehenge, the circle of megalithic stones known worldwide. In 1987, five years after his father died, Reinders and family members created a monument to the man. They painted 39 cars industrial gray and arranged them like Stonehenge. The family dedicated Carhenge on the summer solstice that year with songs and poetry, as the ancient Druids might have.

Carhenge immediately had detractors, but this wasn't a Ford versus Chevy thing. Visible from Nebraska Highway 87 north of Alliance, some considered it an eyesore. But visitors arrived and haven't stopped coming. Carhenge attracts 80,000 visitors annually. The on-site Car Art Reserve includes a dinosaur made of spare parts. The visitor's center is called The Pit Stop. Jim Reinders pulled into that big junkyard in the sky in late 2021. His classic car creation remains at full throttle.

2151 Co. Rd. 59, Alliance, 308-762-3569, carhenge.com

TIP

Brewery 719 is named after locomotive 719, a steam-powered workhorse enshrined near Laing Park in Alliance. I suggest trying Hazy Train IPA.
817 E 3rd St., Alliance, 308-761-2719

MORE ALLIANCE ATTRACTIONS

Sandhills Drive-In features second-run films on a big screen outdoors, just like during the good old days.
2617 Co. Rd. 57, 308-458-7927
sandhillsdrivein.com

Dobby's Frontier Town offers self-guided tours of a village of historic structures rescued by the late Kenneth "Dobby" Lee.
320 E 25th St., 308-762-7157
dobbysfrontiertown.com

Carnegie Arts Center displays art and holds workshops and special events in the community's former Carnegie Library.
204 W 4th St., 308-762-4571
carnegieartscenter.com

Central Park Fountain has entertained with colored, nighttime light displays ever since it was built in 1935 (except during winter).
204 E 10th St., 308-762-2384
visitalliance.com

Nebraska Veterans Cemetery honors our nation's heroes on 20 acres once belonging to the World War II–era Alliance Army Airfield.
2610 Co. Rd. 57, 308-763-2958
veterans.nebraska.gov/nvca

Sandhills Open Road Challenge in Arnold

SPORTS AND RECREATION

SWING A PUTTER
AT THE PRAIRIE CLUB

I'm not a golfer, but when the opportunity came up to play around (not "a round") at this world-class, semi-private Sandhills golf club near Valentine, a friend lent me his putter. The Sandhills offers challenging beauty for those who choose to whack the little white ball. This landscape inspired founder Paul Shock's creation, The Prairie Club. "The great holes were already there," he once said. "God put them there. We just had to find them." Golfers find Shock's minimalist approach to golf course design in the club's Horse, Pines, and Dunes courses. Whether golfers finish hungry or hangry, they have several options for dining. The Canyon Room overlooks Snake River Canyon. The scene is more rustic at the Dunes Saloon and Pines Canteen, and there are options for private dining in the lodge. Visitors enjoy picnics at several Points of Solitude. Whether you're chipping from a natural sand bunker or watching sunset from the 18th green, this Sandhills adventure is above par.

88897 NE Hwy. 97, Valentine, 888-402-1101, theprairieclub.com

TIP

Merritt Trading Post Resort is 9 miles south of The Prairie Club on the shore of Merritt Reservoir.

88337 NE Hwy. 97, Valentine, 402-376-3437

MORE SANDHILLS-AREA GOLF COURSES

Wild Horse Golf Club
Public, 18-hole, par 72
40950 Rd. 768, Gothenburg
308-537-7700
playwildhorse.com

Sand Hills Golf Club
Private, 18-hole, par 71
36410 Sand Hills Rd., Mullen
308-546-2237

Pelican Beach Golf Club
Public, 9-hole, par 36
54057 N NE Hwy. 61, Hyannis
308-458-2579

Bassett Country Club
Public, 9-hole, par 36
W US Hwy. 20, Bassett
402-684-3449
facebook.com/bassettcountryclub

Calamus Golf Course
Public, 9-hole, par 35
82796 Whitetail Ln., Burwell
308-346-5559
facebook.com/calamusgolfcourse

Thedford Golf Course
Public, 9-hole, par 36
39260 Golf Course Ln., Thedford
308-645-7190
golfingnebraska.com

Summerland Golf Club
Public, 9-hole, par 36
51020 857th Rd., Ewing
402-626-7555

Ainsworth Municipal Golf Course
Public, 9-hole, par 36
E US Hwy. 20, Ainsworth
402-387-1658
cityofainsworth.com

Mullen Golf Club
Public, 9-hole, par 36
377 W NE Hwy. 2, Mullen
308-546-2445

Hay Springs Golf Course
Public, 9-hole, par 36
445 Ln., Hay Springs
308-638-7275

Frederick Peak Golf Club
Public, 10-hole, par 39
1000 Dowden St., Valentine
402-322-2754
valentinegolf.com

Sand Ridge Golf Course
Public, 9-hole, par 36
402 E 3rd St., Rushville
308-327-2966

Gordon Country Club and Golf Course
Public, 9-hole, par 36
6535 210th Ln., Gordon
308-282-1146

Augusta Winds Golf Club
Public, 9-hole, par 36
US Hwy. 83, Stapleton
308-529-1861

LOSE YOURSELF
AT SANDHILLS CORN MAZE

J W and Becky Bowen left big-city life in a neighboring state to raise their children in the Sandhills, where the pace is slower. Ainsworth welcomed the Bowens, and now the family welcomes visitors each October to their Sandhills Corn Maze. In a fun way, the maze frustrates visitors who stall at dead ends and get disoriented through twists and turns in the 17-acre field. Giggles and guffaws echo from the rows. Laughing turns to shrieks and screams after sundown, when the attraction morphs into a haunted version.

Other fun includes a sandbox-like corn pit, feed-wagon basketball, duck races, cornhole, a pumpkin patch, decorated hay bales, and a two-lane slide down the elevated bed of a well-worn farm truck. The family attraction run by family and friends adds new activities each year. Happy Halloween!

From west of Ainsworth, go south on 429th Ave. and then turn right (west) on 877th Rd. for less than a mile. Signs point the way.
303-809-3882, facebook.com/sandhillscornmaze

TIP

The Nebraska Sandhills Cowboy Hall of Fame is located at the Palmer Law Group office in Ainsworth.
sandhillscowboys.com

RACK 'EM
AT NEWPORT POOL HALL

Newport was once the Hay Capital of the World. Hay cut in Sandhills meadows was shipped to cities when the world operated on horsepower—that is, before automobiles replaced horses as our chief mode of transportation. The hay grown here today is important for feeding cattle, but the business has changed, and Newport is much smaller than during its hay heyday. The office of one former hay scale stands tall in Newport, which today has about 70 residents. Inside is an attraction I've seen nowhere else in the Sandhills—a 24-hour pool hall.

With original plans of opening a post office, owner Melissa Denny restored the place and even got the hay scale working again. Instead of mail, pool players send solids and stripes rolling into the pockets. The restored 1898 structure has become a popular stop on the Cowboy Trail (#56) with a beverage vending machine and honor-system snacks. That's a win-win, even if you did scratch on the eight-ball.

2nd St., Newport

TIP

Just west of Newport, a Nebraska Historical Marker claims Spring Valley Park as the first roadside rest area in the state. The park still offers weary travelers a safe detour for rest.

SUIT UP FOR FOOTBALL
IN THE SANDHILLS

Football season weather in the Sandhills ranges from summer-hot to winter-white. I suggest packing additional layers when you attend these games. When Friday night lights come up and the sun sets, temps sink, too. More typical, though, are the mild autumn nights that football fans live for. Button up a flannel, grab a bag of concession-stand popcorn, and root for athletes giving it their all.

Most Nebraska schools play 11- or 8-man football. In sparsely populated parts of the state, schools play six-man football, which was invented in Nebraska during the Great Depression. In Thedford, which takes turns hosting Sandhills-Thedford High School home games with Dunning, businesses close early for afternoon eight-man football games. Cowboy hats and seed corn caps come off as the school band plays our national anthem. These Sandhills kids play to win, with school and community pride as important as the final score. Find team information and schedules at nsaahome.org.

TIP

Thedford is headquarters for the Middle Loup River Challenge, a race with divisions for kayaks, canoes, and paddleboards on the Saturday following Labor Day.

sandhillrivertrips.com

DON'T DRIVE LIKE HELL
IN HIDDEN PARADISE

Barely a mile south of Long Pine, cabins flank Long Pine Creek in a resort area known as Hidden Paradise. What began as shacks and modest cabins more than a century ago has grown into larger homes and recreational retreats wedged into the narrow canyon. A sign states this is "a heavenly place," and to "please don't drive like hell."

In a wide spot in the canyon road in 1912, Carlton Pettijohn built his Hidden Paradise dance hall between the creek and a sheer cliff known as Chalk Mountain. Locals still speak of entertainers Lawrence Welk and Tommy Dorsey packing the place. After being closed for nearly two decades, Hidden Paradise Pavilion was resurrected by owners Sandra and Barry Clark with a complete rebuild, including a new kitchen, bar, and beer garden. They pulled nails for months to salvage the original maple dance floor, where visitors now shuffle their feet only yards from the heavenly creek.

10538 Hidden Paradise Rd., Long Pine, 402-880-8764

TIP

Curiosities at the Long Pine Heritage Society and Heritage House Museum include fulgurite, a chunk of Sandhills sand fused by lightning.
199 W 3rd St., Long Pine

WADE FOR FOSSILS
AT HUTTON RANCH

Harold and Louise Hutton were good stewards of their land. Their cattle grew fat on bluestem near the Niobrara River, but the Huttons were known for always leaving grass for the wildlife, too. Wanting to ensure their ranch remained ecologically diverse after their passing, the Huttons gifted their land to Audubon of Kansas. The organization is known for its conservation work and has trustees from Nebraska and other states.

Visitors can spend nights in the Hutton House—which has five bedrooms, a large kitchen, and Wi-Fi—and the Lazy Easy Ranch House, which has many comforts of home, but weak cell phone service. Some friends and I spent a weekend here a few years ago. We posed for a photo with one of the largest cottonwood trees I've ever seen—it took six of us to get our arms around it. Then we waded the cool Niobrara River, where we found fossil fragments tumbled smooth by the current.

88923 453rd Ave., Bassett, 785-537-4385, niobrarasanctuary.org

TIP

Allen's Pizza Place is a family-owned restaurant that knows the secrets of making a proper cheeseburger pizza—one of which is dill pickle slices.
109 Clark St., Bassett, 402-684-2555

TEMPT A TROUT
ON LONG PINE CREEK

Long Pine State Recreation Area covers 153 acres near Long Pine. There are campsites, outhouses, grills, picnic tables, and an archery range. The highlight is Long Pine Creek, winding swiftly through the park's pine-covered canyons. Thousands of adventurers float through the recreation area and nearby Hidden Paradise (#34) on inner tubes each summer. The water is cold. The fishing can be hot.

Trout live in the creek. Most adjacent land is privately owned. The best public access is at Long Pine State Recreation Area, Long Pine Wildlife Management Area, and Pine Glen Wildlife Management Area. I've had these scrappy trout grab jigs and spinners. My favorite bait or lure? I'm not telling, but cast your offering into bends, under logs, and into rocky, deep spots. A Nebraska Park Entry Permit is required on vehicles entering the State Recreation Area.

87770 Willow Ridge Ave., Long Pine
402-684-2921, outdoornebraska.gov/longpine

TIP

The Pines rents inner tubes and rustic cabins on the edge of Long Pine near Long Pine Creek. Lodging is also available across US Hwy. 20 from Long Pine at Pine Valley Resort. Find more Long Pine lodging options and other info at longpinenebraska.com.

SPY ON SHARP-TAILED GROUSE FROM A BLIND

Sharp-tailed grouse populations have dwindled across most of their range. The Sandhills is a stronghold for the species. These drab birds usually blend unnoticed into their grassland habitat. But each spring, sharpies put on a show. Males gather to perform mock combat and intricate "dances" to win mating rights from hens. The females watch as males inflate purplish air sacs on their necks and begin stomping.

Their calls sound almost mechanical. At other times they are catlike. Males face off, jump into the air, bite, and kick. Injuries are rare, but feathers are lost. The arrival of a hawk, coyote, or other predator will flush the birds. They usually return as soon as danger passes. Public grouse viewing blinds are available at the Nebraska National Forest near Halsey, Valentine National Wildlife Refuge near Valentine, and Crescent Lake National Wildlife Refuge north of Oshkosh. People come to Nebraska from around the world to see this Sandhills spectacle.

nebraskabirdingtrails.com

TIP

The Sandhills is home to another grouse species, the greater prairie chicken. Guided prairie chicken and sandhill crane tours are available through Dusty Trails LLC. dustytrails.biz

38

CREATE SPARKS
ON THE NIOBRARA RIVER

This isn't a reference to boats scraping the Niobrara River's rocky bottom. Valentine-area outfitters equip outdoor adventurers for exhilarating Niobrara River floats. One is set apart, literally. Seventeen miles downstream of Valentine in Sparks, Dryland Aquatics outfits river runs, canoe cruises, kayak capers, and inner tube trips. Ed and Louise Heinert own the business and community. Their family makes up the entire population of Sparks. Previous owners Lou and Janet Christiansen were also friends of mine. Lou was a fierce protector of the Niobrara River. Dryland Aquatics is headquartered at Sparks General Store.

The store serves patrons with a post office, groceries, cold drinks, ice, and souvenirs like T-shirts, hats, and fossils. Vintage beer coolers and ancient bison skulls adorn the store. Farm-fresh eggs are sold, and the coffee is always on. Find lodging in the former Sparks School, a bunkhouse, and a campground.

41115 Sparks Rd., Sparks, 402-376-3119, drylandaquatics.com

TIP

A 76-mile stretch of the Niobrara River downstream of Valentine was given National Scenic River status in 1991.

nps.gov

MORE VALENTINE-AREA OUTFITTERS

Niobrara River Ranch
402-890-1245
nrranch.com

Sharp's Outfitters
402-376-2506
sharpsoutfitters.com

Graham Canoe Outfitters
402-376-3708
grahamoutfitters.com

Little Outlaw Canoe Rental
402-376-1822
outlawcanoe.com

Brewers Canoers & Tubers
402-376-2046
brewerscanoers.com

Stan's Landing & Fritz's Island Campground
402-432-2568
fritzsislandcampground.com

Rock Barn Outfitters
402-322-0463
rockbarnoutfitters.com

Prairie River Outfitters & Sunny Brook Camp
402-376-1887
facebook.com/sunny.brook.camp

Rocky Ford Camp & Outfitters
402-497-3479
rockyfordcampandoutfitters.com

Heartland Tubes
402-389-1964
facebook.com/heartlandtubes

IMMERSE YOURSELF IN NATURE'S SHOWER

AT SMITH FALLS STATE PARK

Waterfalls in Nebraska? Heck, yeah. There are more than 200 downstream of Valentine along the Niobrara River alone. The highest Nebraska waterfall is Smith Falls, which drops 63 feet. The state park named for it is a convenient stop for adventurers floating the Niobrara River (#38). Many beach their craft and take the boardwalk to the falls. Park visitors walk across the river on the historic Verdigre Bridge.

If you cool off under this refreshing cascade, please don't use soap, shampoo, or other products that could harm this delicate ecosystem. The visitor center displays fossils and sells drinks and snacks. Tent camping is allowed. Explore this unique area on the Jim McAllister Nature Trail. Downstream of Smith Falls, the landing at Brewer Bridge is maintained by the Middle Niobrara Natural Resources District.

90165 Smith Falls Rd., Valentine, 402-376-1306, outdoornebraska.gov

TIP

Snake River Falls, the largest Nebraska waterfall, is a 54-foot-wide cascade on the Snake River between Valentine and Merritt Reservoir. Approximately 23 miles southwest of Valentine on Nebraska Hwy. 97.

40

FEEL SMALL
AT NEBRASKA'S LARGEST LAKE

An Ogallala landmark since the dedication of Kingsley Dam in 1941, Lake McConaughy offers 100 miles of shoreline to those craving sugar-sand beaches. Crocodiles, sea turtles, whales, and other critters get beached on that sand, along with elaborate sandcastles, during the annual Kites & Castles event in July.

Exhibits at the Lake McConaughy Visitor and Water Interpretive Center explain the geology and hydrology of the lake and North Platte River Valley. "Big Mac" is known for its catches of big walleyes. The community of Lemoyne was relocated to build the reservoir. When the water is low, foundations from the former village are seen. When whitecaps whip up, many boaters head to Lake Ogallala. Known as "Ogallala's Little Lake," its sheltered location below McConaughy keeps it mostly out of the wind. Lake Ogallala is famous for the trout prowling its canal. For a taste of local lake culture, visit Van's Lakeview Fishing Camp, a lakeside landmark since 1966.

1475 NE Hwy. 61 N, Ogallala
308-284-8800, outdoornebraska.gov/lakemcconaughy

TIP

Vogl's Lodge & Lure is a bait and tackle shop with cabin rentals on the north shore of Lake McConaughy.
721 Hwy. 92 W, Lemoyne, 308-355-2321, voglslodgeandlure.com

41

MEANDER
THROUGH VALENTINE NATIONAL WILDLIFE REFUGE

Much of the Sandhills appears almost like it did pre-settlement. But to protect one special, 71,516-acre complex of wetlands, uplands, and lakes, the government created the Valentine National Wildlife Refuge in 1935. An incredible 270 bird species have been documented here, and 22 species of reptiles and amphibians, too. Even though this is a wildlife refuge, limited hunting opportunities exist here, and fishing is allowed in some refuge lakes. Yield to the critters crossing the roads here, and don't pick them up. Removing wildlife, plants, fossils, or cultural items from a National Wildlife Refuge is a crime, and refuge staff are watching.

Travelers experience beautiful views from the Little Hay Road self-guided auto route, and from atop the observation tower at the west end of Hackberry Lake. Some paths are open to four-wheel-drive vehicles only—ignore the signs at your own peril. You might see box turtles and an occasional bullsnake at ground level, and majestic trumpeter swans gliding overhead.

39679 Pony Lake Rd., Valentine, 402-376-1889, fws.gov/refuge/valentine

SANDHILLS WINTER EVENTS

Cork Thornton Memorial Ice Fishing Tournament
January, Merritt Reservoir, Valentine

Heart City Bull Bash
February, Main St., Valentine

Polar Bear Tank Race
March, Glidden Canoe Rental, Mullen

Christmas at Bowring Ranch
December, Bowring Ranch State Historical Park, Merriman

Christmas Festival
December, Knight Museum and Sandhills Center, Alliance

Christmas Lighting Contest
December, Ainsworth

Trail of Lights
December, Lake Ericson, Ericson

Dunning Christmas Extravaganza
December, Community Hall, Dunning

Parade of Lights
December, Atkinson

Christmas at the Codys'
December, Buffalo Bill Ranch State Historical Park, North Platte

Christmas Parade of Lights
December, Bassett

Merry Prairie Christmas
December, Mansion on the Hill, Ogallala

Annual Holiday Extravaganza
December, Loup County Event Center, Taylor

HOOK TRANQUILITY
AT PIBEL LAKE RECREATION AREA

Pibel Lake has been special to me since childhood. The 24-acre lake formed during creation of an irrigation dam on Clear Creek in the 1890s. More than 125 years later, Pibel Lake remains a popular recreation destination. The Lower Loup Natural Resources District recently installed new restrooms, fishing piers, and playground equipment near the south shore of the 72-acre park, and a footbridge and walking trail to the north. The agency is planning more improvements. Camping is permitted. So is ice fishing.

Warm-season anglers casting toward logs coax strikes from largemouth bass. Bobbers bob for big bluegills. Channel catfish prowl the lake bottom. Ancient snapping turtles, reportedly older than the lake, sometimes steal the bait. If fishermen pray for big catches, it couldn't hurt to cast toward the western shore, where Pibel Bible Camp has been a fixture since 1939. To the east, Pibel Pleasant Hill Cemetery overlooks this tranquil place of rest and recreation.

9 miles south of Bartlett on US Hwy. 281, then 1 mile east on 823rd Rd.
308-728-3221, llnrd.org/recreation

TIP

Lake Ericson is another childhood haunt of mine where bass, bluegill, perch, pike, catfish, and carp are hooked. Camping is allowed near where Buller Trail parallels the west side of the lake, south of Ericson.

43

LOOP
THROUGH THE LOUP RIVERS SCENIC BYWAY

Many people dread their daily commute. Not me—I travel nearly 40 miles of this byway most days. Beginning on Nebraska Highway 11 at Wood River, it stretches through farmland to Burwell, where it doglegs west on Nebraska Highway 91. Favorite stops include Dannebrog Delights ice cream and Danish Bakery pizza on Thursday evenings. Both are in Dannebrog. Continue north to Happy Jack Peak and Chalk Mine, with more than a mile of underground tunnels. A building made of the chalk still stands in Scotia.

The byway continues past Main Street Gallery in North Loup, Valley County Museum in Ord, Calamus Reservoir (#45), the Taylor Villagers (#82), the unincorporated community of Almeria, and the village of Brewster, and ends at Dunning. A one-room school in Burwell serves as the byway's visitor center.

loupriversscenicbyway.org

TIP

Travelers find comfortable, pet-friendly lodging for up to six people at Brando's Bunkhouse in Dunning, 308-430-0786. Find Taylor-area lodging at taylorne.com/lodging, and Burwell-area stays at visitburwell.com/accommodations/lodging.

FLOAT THROUGH THE SANDHILLS
IN A COW WATER TANK

Military tanks are few in the Sandhills, but an armada of livestock water tanks navigate Sandhills streams. Legend has it that the wind tumbled an empty livestock tank to the riverbank, a curious cowpoke climbed in, and "tanking" was born. Bruce Switzer won't admit to being that cowboy, but each year his family's ecotourism business, Calamus Outfitters, launches thousands of adventurers downstream in tanks and on inner tubes on the Calamus River.

The shallow stream has a sandy bottom and is flanked with wildlife, grazing cattle, and the enormous Sandhills sky. Tanks are stable and safe, but difficult to row, so let Mother Nature do the work. Pack sunscreen, snacks, and drinks, and you're set for the leisurely Sandhills adventure of a lifetime. Two- and four-hour trips are available. You can also experience the Sandhills with a guided, off-road tour of this fifth-generation Nebraska cattle ranch.

83720 Valleyview Ave., Burwell, 308-346-4697, calamusoutfitters.com

TIP

Calamus Outfitters lodging is available in two lodges and four cabins.

MORE TANKING OUTFITTERS

Get Tanked LLC (Cedar River)
82379 Ericson-Scotia Ave., Ericson, 308-750-5974
facebook.com/therealgettanked

Crazy Rayz Tanking (Cedar River)
82228 499th Ave., Spalding, 308-571-0990
rbernt@yahoo.com

Dusty Trails LLC (North Platte River)
2617 N Buffalo Bill Ave., North Platte, 308-530-0048
dustytrails.biz

Glidden Canoe Rental (#55) (Middle Loup River)
Mullen, 308-546-2207
gliddencanoerental.com

Sandhill River Trips (Middle Loup River)
608 Court St., Thedford, 308-645-2235
sandhillrivertrips.com

SLICE AND DICE

PUMPKINS AT CALAMUS RESERVOIR

In addition to 31 miles of sandy beaches, Calamus Reservoir is a recreational destination known for catfish, wiper, and pike fishing. But the fun doesn't drain from the 5,123-acre lake when summer changes to autumn. Each year in late October, Homestead Knolls Campground fills with RVs, pumpkins, and creative pumpkin carvers of all ages.

Carvers carve from morning to afternoon. Games include the Downhill Pumpkin Rolling Derby, and pumpkin and gourd launching at the boat dock. As the sun seems to set into the lake, the jack-o-lanterns are arranged in an illuminated display. As visitors peruse the pumpkin creations, children trick-or-treat from camper to decorated camper. The annual Pumpkin Carvers Event began when an area resident brought four pumpkins to a family camping trip in the late 1980s. Since then, it's grown into a veritable pumpkin patch of orange gourds meeting the knife's edge in anticipation of Halloween. Nebraska Park Entry Permit required.

42285 York Pt. Rd., Burwell, 308-346-5666, outdoornebraska.gov

TIP

Of course, Calamus State Fish Hatchery doesn't grow pumpkins, but the staff does raise walleye, yellow perch, channel catfish, muskellunge, and black crappie. Rainbow trout reared here are stocked statewide.

42254 Hatchery Rd., Burwell, 308-346-4226

RACE A DUCK
FOR ANSELMO'S BIG SKY JUBILEE

The Nebraska Sandhills could rightly claim the title of Big Sky Country. In 1967, Anselmo created its annual Big Sky Jubilee. The three-day June celebration includes a ranch rodeo, softball, horseshoe tournaments, and a pancake feed where members of the Anselmo-Merna School Board flip the flapjacks. There's also a parade. One recent parade poked fun at Nebraska's tourism slogan with the theme of "Anselmo, It's Not For Everybody." Local firefighters light up a barbecue and watermelon feed at the fire hall after the scavenger hunt. The street dance rocks until 2 a.m.!

Later in the summer, organizers hold a duck race beginning at Milburn Diversion Dam Wildlife Management Area. Participants float down the Middle Loup River on canoes, kayaks, paddleboards, tanks, and inner tubes before releasing a flock of 200 plastic ducklings. The first duck passing under Milburn Bridge is the winner. The event raises funds for the next Big Sky Jubilee celebration.

facebook.com/anselmonebraska

TIP

While in Anselmo, make sure to check out the historic, 1800s jail and the sod house on Smith Avenue.

custertourism.com/anselmo

REV UP
AT STUART RACEWAY

As weekends brake to a halt, Sunday evenings rev up in Stuart. Stock cars have raced here since 1953 at what the community proudly claims is "the oldest consecutively run racetrack in the US with all-volunteer help." Whew! The stands are already filling when hot laps begin at 6:15 p.m. Racing begins at 7 p.m. The mixed aroma of popcorn, racing fuel, and adrenaline drifts on the Sandhills breeze. The May-to-August races feature hobby stock, sprint, winged, stock non-wing, and other classes. Drivers jockey for position on the quarter-mile clay oval track north of US Highway 20 and adjacent to Stuart Community Park.

The track lights come up as the sun sets. I suggest napping earlier in the day so you don't miss exciting races that could last late into the night. Better bring your ear plugs, too. At more than 70 years old, Stuart Raceway doesn't show any signs of slowing down anytime soon.

702 E 2nd St., Stuart, 402-340-1634, stuartraceway.myracepass.com

TIP

The White Horse Museum and Heritage Village celebrates area history and the American Albino horses from the White Horse Ranch north of Stuart that performed across the US starting in 1938.

203 S Main St., Stuart, 402-924-3168

MAKE HAY
IN ATKINSON

Nebraska's farmers and ranchers harvested 6.3 million tons of hay in 2022. Atkinson, located in the fertile Elkhorn River Valley, is proud of its hay heritage. So proud, in fact, that they take a break from farm and ranch work briefly each August to celebrate Hay Days. If you miss the sign welcoming you to town, the decorated hay bales dotting the community let you know you're in the right prairie place. Prizes are awarded for the best-decorated hay bale sculptures.

The Hay Days king and queen are crowned, a parade marches through town, and carnivores chow down at the Ribs Showcase. Smoke rolls from the burnout contest, the cakewalk happens in Atkinson City Park (there's a pie walk, too), and the duck races have people flocking to downtown. Atkinson residents hope you'll stop by and say, "Hay!"

atkinsonhaydays.com

TIP

Swan Lake is located about halfway between Atkinson and Burwell on Nebraska Highway 11. I've never seen a swan there, but this lake shines with catches of bluegill and yellow perch during ice-fishing season.

STICK AROUND STAPLETON

This Sandhills community has Nebraska's "good life" figured out. With a population of 267 only 30 miles from North Platte, Stapleton could have declined into ghost-town status. Residents wouldn't have it. The Stapleton Chamber of Commerce boasts 52 members, and the community has several Airbnbs and campgrounds, two boutiques, and a community-owned grocery store. And there is something unbelievable downtown.

When modernization left the *Stapleton Enterprise* with empty press rooms, the publisher surveyed residents about what need that space could fill. Turns out they longed to sample fine wine and whiskeys. Herbie's Speakeasy was born. Tasting events take place in what residents say is the only combination newspaper office/liquor store on earth. Each August, Stapleton hosts the Logan County Fair. There's a pulled pork barbecue, sand volleyball, food vendors, games, a bake sale, and a rodeo. Youngins cling to sheep in the Mutton Bustin' event. I like watching the Stick Horse Barrel Races. Reminds me to stick around Stapleton more often.

stapleton-ne.com

TIP

Stapleton's spiritual needs are served by Catholic and Presbyterian churches. Gandy, two miles east of Stapleton, is home to Gandy Community Bible Church.

ACCELERATE YOUR NEED FOR SPEED

IN ARNOLD

The Sandhills Open Road Challenge began in 2001 as a one-day road race with 34 drivers. The annual event has accelerated into a Sandhills speed spectacular, with more than 120 drivers and three race events. Drivers piloting Corvettes, Camaros, Mustangs, Lamborghinis, and other high-performance rides follow Dunning Road out of the South Loup River Valley, across Judkins Table, and into the Sandhills. Then they race back.

This isn't side-by-side racing. Drivers launch one by one for the best time in their category. Drivers in the 120-miles-per-hour class hope to end their 55-mile run with an average speed of 120 miles per hour. S-curves and 90-degree turns slow them down, which means making up time in straightaways with speeds up to 140 miles per hour. Crossing deer occasionally slow the action. Other activities include a parade, car show, barbecue, and a street dance. The Chicken Noodle Dinner is served until it's gone.

308-848-2522, sorcrace.com

TIP

The One-Mile Shootout, with a record of 224.77 mph, takes place on the Cozad/Callaway County Rd. The Loup 2 Loup Open Road Race races cars on 12 miles of rural asphalt between Purdum and Halsey.

SEE THE STARS
AT MERRITT RESERVOIR

In terms of light pollution, the Nebraska Sandhills is one of the darkest places on earth. Milky Way views here are stunning, even more so when the spiral galaxy is reflected in the waters of Merritt Reservoir south of Valentine. The altitude here, combined with the Sandhills' dry conditions, means high atmospheric transparency.

Each July, Snake River Area Campground becomes the NASA of Nebraska, as astronomers and stargazers of every level arrive for the Nebraska Star Party. No telescope? No problem. I've always found participants happy to share their equipment and knowledge, and the Beginner's Field School teaches everything needed for newbies looking to enjoy the night sky. During the day, when these stargazers should be sleeping, many rest their tired eyes on Merritt's sandy beaches, explore Valentine National Wildlife Refuge (#41) or float the Niobrara River (#38). Most catch a little shuteye before sundown.

Merritt Reservoir is 26 miles south of Valentine on Nebraska Hwy. 97.
402-333-5460, nebraskastarparty.org

TIP

Valentine visitors explore the Simmons Ranch during guided tours at Golden Prairie Bison.
402-606-1127, goldenprairiebison.com

52

HUNT FOR THE MONSTER
OF WALGREN LAKE

Could a dragon-like behemoth slumber in the mucky bottom of this usually quiet lake near the edge of the Sandhills? Tales of such a creature have circulated for more than a century. In 1923, resident J. A. Johnson told newspapers that he and dozens of other witnesses saw a grayish-brown monster in the lake. He estimated it to be 40 feet long. With a horn between its eyes and nostrils, and described as alligator-like, the animal let out a roar, Johnson said. And then, with a splash of its rudderlike-tail, the beast was gone. Skeptics suggested the creature was an unusually large beaver. Other accounts give the animal glowing green eyes and a hunger for Sandhills cattle.

Today, Walgren Lake State Recreation Area is a peaceful escape for man and beast. There's a shaded campground and picnic areas, a boat dock, and a playground. Huge panfish lurk in the 50-acre lake. Maybe someday, someone will hook a true monster. Nebraska Park Entry Permit and sense of adventure required.

4175 540th Rd., Hay Springs
308-432-6167, outdoornebraska.gov/walgrenlake

TIP

Heritage Center Museums 1 and 2 preserve local history.
133 N Main St., Hay Springs

SADDLE UP
AT NEBRASKA'S BIG RODEO

2021 marked the 100th year of this cherished, small-town rodeo, but it's not a small rodeo. Up to 18,000 people turn out over the course of the four-day event. Cowboys and cowgirls from across the nation follow the Pro Rodeo Cowboys Association tour to Burwell with hopes of sticking winning rides. Locals get in on the action, especially during the Wild Horse Race.

Pickups hauling trailers roar into the arena. Trailer doors swing open, horses bolt, and teams of three must catch their animal, strap a saddle on its back, and mount a rider. The first team to send horse and rider around one lap is the winner. Horse hooves occasionally hit their mark during the melee, leaving cowboys breathless or worse. Coinciding with the Garfield County Fair, the celebration includes parades, dances, livestock exhibits, food vendors, beer gardens, games, and herds of Sandhills hospitality.

46710 L St., Burwell, 308-346-5010, nebraskasbigrodeo.com

TIP

Not in Burwell during the rodeo? Check out the Northside Bar & Café, Nebraska's only combination rodeo museum and bar.

223 Grand Ave., Burwell, 308-346-5474

HELP A TURTLE
CROSS A SANDHILLS ROAD

Because ranching has a mostly gentle impact on the Sandhills, the region is a stronghold for at-risk species. As nesting season approaches, large numbers of turtles are on the move. If a road crosses a turtle's migration route, tragedy can occur. The fragmented remains of turtles litter some stretches of Nebraska asphalt. I know from experience that family members won't appreciate you running in front of traffic to save turtles. But these animals usually can be safely moved out of harm's way.

Experts say to move turtles off roads only if it is safe to do so—watch for cars—and always move them in the direction they were going. Keep in mind that Nebraska law prohibits relocating reptiles more than 100 yards from where they were captured. These long-lived animals do poorly in captivity. Please leave them in the wild Sandhills where they belong. Bring home a photo as a souvenir instead. Oh, and those feisty snapping turtles aren't aggressive, but can get defensive when approached.

outdoornebraska.gov/turtles

TIP

The Twisted Turtle Pub in Rushville is famous for brick-oven pizzas. The Sandhill Surfer is loaded with brisket, barbecue sauce, onions, and pineapple.

129 Main St., Rushville, 308-327-2233

PADDLE
THE MIDDLE LOUP RIVER

Mitch Glidden, co-owner of Glidden Canoe Rental with his wife, Patty, is so busy launching kayakers, canoeists, and tankers downstream spring, summer, and fall, that winter is the only time he gets to float his own boat. He came to appreciate the quieter cold season, but didn't keep winter tanking to himself. Being the sharing Sandhillers they are, the Gliddens founded the Polar Bear Tank Race as a fundraiser for the Sandhills Journey National Scenic Byway. Not sure what tanking is? See #44.

It's still cold here during the first weekend of March. That's when adventurers from Nebraska and neighboring states meet in Mullen, the only incorporated community in Hooker County, for a river race like no other. Teams of four to six float, paddle, and push their stock tanks down the four-mile course. The record, held by the local River Ratts team, is 56 minutes and 57 seconds. Already cold thinking about the race? A soup feed the night before cranks up the heat.

Glidden Canoe Rental
308-546-2207, gliddencanoerental.com

TIP

Lodging is available nearby at Double R Guest Ranch, 308-546-2376, and at Sandhills Motel, 308-546-2206.

MORE IN MULLEN

Mullen Arts Center features the creations of local artists and conducts art workshops and special events. Home of the Meadowlark Market.
109 NW 1st St., 308-546-0636

Hondo Lanes offers open bowling, children's bowling with bumpers, and fall and winter league bowling.
202 S Washington St., 308-546-2417

Red's Cafe & Lounge is a roadside diner and bar wedged between railroad tracks and Nebraska Hwy. 2.
404 SW 1st St., 308-546-2770

Chuckwagon 'n Jug is known for generous servings of burgers, pizzas, and other goodies. Ask about the Rancher's Special.
201 S Lincoln Ave., 308-546-2284

FOLLOW
THE COWBOY TRAIL

This rails-to-trail conversion stretches 187 miles from Norfolk to Valentine. Much of the route—surfaced with crushed limestone—leads hikers, bicyclists, and horseback riders through the northern Sandhills. The scenery is stunning. In most stretches, there is a town every 10 to 15 miles. Several of these communities are small with few available services, so plan and pack carefully, especially if planning to take the trail start to finish. Plans to complete the trail to Chadron have slowed, but an additional 15 miles is now complete between Gordon and Rushville, thanks to local volunteers. Sandburs and flat tires are common—bring extra tubes if biking.

The former railroad bridge east of Valentine is a quarter-mile long and crosses 148 feet over the Niobrara River—talk about a view! Last time I was on this bridge, a turkey vulture let me get unusually close before spiraling into the thermals. Maybe the scavenger was hoping I wouldn't make it to the trail's end.

402-471-0641, outdoornebraska.gov/cowboytrail

TIP

North Fork Outfitting offers Cowboy Trail Adventure vacation packages, including shuttle service between Norfolk and Valentine.
402-316-0157, nforkoutfitting.com

57

DISCOVER THE FOREST
IN A SEA OF GRASS

The undulating grasslands forming the Sandhills region has been called a prairie sea. But there are trees here. The Nebraska National Forest is tucked between the Dismal and Middle Loup rivers near Halsey and Thedford. In 1902, based on input from the University of Nebraska's Dr. Charles Bessey, President Theodore Roosevelt established the Dismal River Forest Reserve. It became the Nebraska National Forest and grew to become the largest hand-planted forest in the western hemisphere. Approximately 22,000 acres of the 90,445-acre reserve is forested. The rest is rolling sand hills.

Recreational opportunities include upland bird hunting, big-game hunting, fishing, ATV riding, camping, horseback riding, wildlife photography, and birding. The annual 4-H Foundation Trail Ride brings people together under the pines each October. Sandhills ranchers donate hay harvested from this ocean of grass.

40637 River Loop Rd., Halsey, 308-533-0427, fs.usda.gov

TIP

Georg Joutras's 2018 documentary, *Ocean of Grass: Life on a Nebraska Sandhills Ranch*, chronicles the McGinn family and their ranch near Dunning.

oceanofgrassfilm.com

DRINK IN
THE FOUNTAIN OF YOUTH AT VICTORIA SPRINGS

Founded in 1925 on the former townsite of New Helena, Victoria Springs State Recreation Area is Nebraska's third-oldest state park. Little remains of the community, founded near a crystal-clear spring, but the park does preserve two log cabins. One was Custer County's first post office. The other was home to postmaster and judge Charles R. Matthews. After hearing legends comparing Victoria Spring water to the mythical Fountain of Youth, Matthews and other investors formed Victoria Mineral Springs Company. In 1890, they began bottling the water, but the venture never took off. The population drained when the railroad bypassed New Helena for nearby Anselmo. Matthews left, too.

A footbridge links the park with the campground across Victoria Creek. A Nebraska Park Entry Permit is required for vehicles to enter, and campers must pay a fee. Although bottling the spring water didn't pan out, Victoria Springs offers respite for those who drink it in.

43400 NE Hwy. S 21A, Anselmo, 308-749-2235, outdoornebraska.gov

TIP

On the eastern edge of Merna, Downey Well Company displays 31 vintage windmills and plans to add more.

399 W Old NE Hwy. 2, Merna

WATCH SANDHILL CRANES
ALONG THE NORTH PLATTE RIVER

Each spring, south central Nebraska welcomes the world's largest congregation of cranes. That's not the Sandhills, but 150 miles west of Kearney, the Sandhill Crane Capital of the World, the Nebraska Sandhills presents a crane spectacle of its own.

From mid-February through mid-April, cranes gather along the North Platte River. Flocks can be seen from rural roads, but one special place is the Old Lewellen Bridge south of Lewellen. The road is narrow. Please be courteous to motorists and respect private land. This is not a zoo. Viewing is permitted from a very small pullout near the bridge. On my first visit, there were thousands of cranes, myself, and four members of a Lakota family. As the sun sank, wave after wave of cranes flew over and landed in the safety of the shallow river. The spectacle was especially meaningful to these Native Americans: the river, the cranes, and the Sandhills are sacred to their tribe. Please treat these marvels of nature as if sacred to you, too.

308-778-9557

TIP

The Most Unlikely Place (#98) is sandhill crane central. The art gallery, cafe, and performance venue in Lewellen holds special events during the crane migration and offers tips to birders. themostunlikelyplace.com

Lakeland Sod High School marker near Long Lake, Brown County.

CULTURE AND HISTORY

PAINT THE WORLD'S LARGEST SHAMROCK
IN O'NEILL

O'Neill became the Irish Capital of Nebraska in 1969. Settlers from the Emerald Isle arrived here nearly 100 years earlier. The community remembers its roots with a celebration lasting the better part of a week. People line the parade route, a pony dyed green canters along Douglas Street, and the Irish Dancers . . . dance. Then there's my favorite of the festivities—the painting of the World's Largest Shamrock.

The intersection of US highways 20 and 281 is closed as attendees gather where a three-leaf clover is etched in the pavement. Then, rollers soaked in green paint are handed to children. They take turns painting. While working on this book in 2022, I was surrounded with green paint while I shot photos. The luck of the Irish was with me—they kindly left me a way out! In my opinion, this is one of the best community celebrations in the Sandhills and all of Nebraska.

402-336-3640, cityofoneillnebraska.com

TIP

In O'Neill, people gather at Handlebend Tap, known for Moscow Mules served in copper mugs made here in the backroom workshop of the historic Shelhamer Building. Handlebend also pours Nebraska craft beers, mixed drinks, and wine.

215 E Douglas St., O'Neill, 402-340-2983, handlebend.com

HORSE AROUND
AT KNIGHT MUSEUM AND SANDHILLS CENTER

Museums in Sandhills communities do a wonderful job of preserving local history. The Knight Museum and Sandhills Center stands alone when it comes to interpreting Sandhills culture.

Inside stands a fiberglass filly. The faux foal came to Alliance in 1909 to model harnesses and saddles at Newberry's Hardware Company. The horse, named Newberry, became a cherished local resident. The animal is stabled today in the state-of-the-art museum that reopened in 2010 after a massive renovation. The museum's mission to "preserve, honor, and educate others about the history of Alliance and Western Nebraska and about the Sandhills pioneer spirit" is evident in exhibits featuring Native Americans, the Sandhills, and the railroad. I was exploring the basement archives years ago when museum director Becci Thomas showed me a bowl of jelly crafted by a pioneer woman in 1871. Thomas was only horsing around when she offered me a taste. Other sweets and souvenirs are available in the museum's Newberry Gift Shop.

908 Yellowstone Ave., Alliance, 308-762-2384, knightmuseum.com

TIP

Newberry's Common Ground Coffee Café serves up hot and cold beverages, breakfast, lunch, and baked goods.
402 Box Butte Ave., Alliance, 308-761-1300

LIGHT CHRISTMAS CANDLES
AT DRY VALLEY CHURCH

Electricity didn't reach some parts of the Sandhills until the 1950s. It never reached Dry Valley Church. That doesn't keep the glow of Christmas from shining from this country church, northwest of Mullen in southern Cherry County.

Dedicated in 1912, this little house of worship on the prairie was built of blocks made from local blowout sand. Services ceased in 1958. The church was in sad shape in 1986, when a desperate letter printed in the *Hooker County Tribune* inspired volunteers to save it. There's no weekly worship, but visitors have attended a sunset service here the Sunday of Memorial Day weekend since 1988. Neighbors, which rancher Judy Ridenour says live mostly in a 30-mile radius, also gather for Christmas. She organizes the Christmas Candlelight Service that begins with children lighting candelabra made of horseshoes by a local man. Singing and readings end with "Silent Night," "The Lord's Prayer," and fellowship with coffee and cookies, before attendees head their separate ways through the Sandhills by starlight.

14 miles north of Mullen on NE Hwy. 97, then 3 miles west, 308-546-2626

TIP

The Pilgrim Holiness Church in Arthur, which now belongs to the Arthur County Historical Society, was built out of straw bales in 1928. The organization's museum, once the smallest courthouse in the United States, is also in Arthur. 308-764-2203

63

EXPAND YOUR ARTISTIC HORIZONS
AT THEDFORD ART GALLERY

I know a lot of Sandhillers who are amazingly creative. Some of the best artistic creations from the region are featured at Thedford Art Gallery. A volunteer here once told me that anything with a windmill on it will sell. There are plenty of windmills, horses, cattle, cowboys, ranch scenes, wildlife, yucca plants, and sunrises and sunsets in this homey gallery on the north side of Nebraska Highway 2. Each room of the former home is stocked with works of art. A large gallery in the back doubles as space for art shows and receptions, and for art workshops for children and adults.

The galleries here are filled with photos, paintings, sculpture, jewelry, and works of other mediums, many of which are inspired by ranching, the American West, life in Nebraska, and the Sandhills—the most beautiful canvas of all.

509 Court St., Thedford, 308-645-2586, facebook.com/thedfordartgallery

TIP

Local art hangs in the Sandhills Corral restaurant in Thedford.
39359 NE Hwy. 2, Thedford, 308-645-2323

SOAR WITH THE SAVIDGE BROTHERS IN EWING

Ingenuity. It's a trait common to Sandhillers and most Nebraskans, but perhaps the Savidge family members had more than their fair share. On their Holt County farm near Ewing, they built a small-scale railway to haul kitchen scraps to the hogs and created a dog-powered treadmill to churn butter and wash clothes. Brothers Phil, John, Dave, Joe, Louis, Matt, and George even enlisted the family's one-eyed cat as a volunteer for their efforts in aviation, strapping the feline onto a homemade glider rolled down the barn roof.

The brothers learned to fly and then barnstormed across the Great Plains. Matt Savidge has been credited with inventing skywriting. On June 17, 1916, he achieved another first—he was the first Nebraskan to die in an airplane crash in the state. Ninety-four years later, after I nominated Matt and his brothers, they were inducted into the Nebraska Aviation Hall of Fame. The soaring Savidge Brothers are not forgotten. A downtown Ewing mural shows their biplane soaring over a Sandhills meadow.

E Nebraska and N Cedar Streets, Ewing

TIP

Duane Hutchinson's book, *Sandhills Aviators*, provides an entertaining chronicle of the brothers from Ewing and their family's many achievements on the ground and above.

REDISCOVER THE BRONZE AGE IN BARTLETT

Seeing cowboys is expected in Bartlett. But on the south side of town, one nine-foot-tall cowboy has people looking up. The bronze statue of a rider and horse named *Silent Leather* towers over the Wheeler County Historical Society's Courthouse Museum grounds and what locals claim is the largest Western-themed sculpture garden in the United States. Forty-three bronzes, all created by Bartlett native artist Herb Mignery, occupy the museum lawn. When I drive by the Mignery Sculpture Garden, resident Bob Nichols is often there shining statues or talking with visitors. I've known Nichols since spending my summers in Bartlett when I was a kid. He's known Mignery since they were boys.

Oh, and as for the "largest Western-themed sculpture garden" claim, "That's what we're saying until someone proves us wrong," Nichols said. He estimates having met 25,000 people in the sculpture garden and told me that Bartlett has more bronze sculptures per capita of any town in the world: "one for about every three residents." More bronzes are planned.

3rd and Main Streets, Bartlett, 308-654-3308

TIP

The Stone House, a mansion built for a Chicago millionaire more than a century ago, stands northeast of Bartlett on Stone House Ave. Arrange tours via thestonehouse1906@gmail.com.

TRAVEL BACK IN TIME
AT BOWRING RANCH

Eva Kelly's car broke down in the Sandhills in 1928. Local cattleman Arthur Bowring happened upon the stranded woman and offered help, as any Sandhills rancher would. Romance bloomed like sand milkweed, and they married. Mr. Bowring was politically active, serving locally and at the state and national levels. In 1954, his wife became Nebraska's first-ever female US senator. She operated the ranch for 41 years after her husband's passing, until her own death in 1985. Bowring gifted their Bar 99 Ranch to the people of Nebraska.

Bowring Ranch State Historical Park remains a working ranch. Home furnishings include collections of glassware, china, and silver. The visitor center interprets Sandhills settlement and ranching. The park hosts Sod House Saturday Night with a barbecue supper, open-mic entertainment, and a dance in the parking lot, surrounded by sandy hills.

90468 NE Hwy. 61, Merriman
308-684-3428, outdoornebraska.gov/location/bowring-ranch

TIP

Cottonwood Lake State Recreation Area is located just east of Merriman and offers camping, fishing, peace, quiet, and Sandhills solitude.
outdoornebraska.gov

SETTLE IN
AT BASSETT LODGE & RANGE CAFE

Bassett Lodge occupies a huge bootprint along Clark Street in Bassett. With origins to 1925, the hotel was expanded and reopened in 1951 to cater to high-dollar cattle buyers. They came to Bassett from as far away as Chicago to attend the town's livestock sales. An extravagant banquet before each sale treated the high rollers like royalty, which helped the hotel earn the nickname, the Cattleman's Castle. Partying stretched into the night, with basement poker games often lasting until dawn. The hotel had the reputation for the most luxurious lodging available between Chicago and Denver. Many of the rooms have been modernized, but the lodge retains its original, opulent Western feel.

A large cattle drive photo hangs above the lunch counter and 12 spinner stools in the attached Range Cafe. Nebraska beef is featured on the menu. Hang your cap on the bull horn hat rack near the door and settle in.

205 Clark St., Bassett, 402-684-3379, bassettlodge.com

TIP

The Rock County Historical Society Museum features six buildings preserving the history of Bassett and Rock County. Includes a country school, church, and Bassett's historic Chicago & North Western Railroad depot.

507 S Park St., Bassett, 402-760-0642

TRACK AL CAPONE
TO THE HISTORIC GOLDEN HOTEL

TV host Geraldo Rivera didn't find Chicago gangster Al Capone's loot, but what did Scarface leave in tunnels under O'Neill in the 1920s? Legend has it that Capone laundered illegal funds through O'Neill businesses and avoided law enforcement by traveling the tunnels under city streets. Christine Carman, owner of the Historic Golden Hotel, doesn't believe it. "He was the type to arrive with an entourage of guards," she said. "He didn't need to hide." Still, when I asked about the subterranean labyrinth, Carman showed me. We didn't find anything, either. The former steam tunnels are mostly filled in.

She decorates the lobby with snapshots of Capone. The Golden was the most opulent lodging around in Capone's day. Carman says it's likely he stayed there when visiting his Nebraska relatives. She's felt an eerie presence here but doesn't believe it was the gangster ghost of one-time Public Enemy No. 1.

406 E Douglas St., O'Neill, 402-336-4436, historicgoldenhotel.com

TIP

Uncover more history at the Moses P. Kinkaid Museum.
401 E Douglas St., O'Neill, 402-608-6933

FIND
THEDFORD'S LOST LITTLE GIRLS

Getting lost in the Sandhills can be easy. Unthinkable tragedy became a nightmare for the Haumann family in 1891 when daughters Anna, "Retta," and Matilda, "Tillie," became lost while walking home from a nearby ranch. With few natural landmarks and having lived in the area for only two months, the sisters lost their bearings. A search party was organized. Four-year-old Retta was found alive three days later, about 25 miles from home. Several more days passed before Tillie's lifeless remains were discovered near Dunning. She wandered an estimated 75 miles before perishing.

Six generations of the Haumann family gathered in 2016 for the dedication of a Nebraska Historical Marker memorializing the tragedy. The monument stands in the Thomas County Courthouse lawn in Thedford. Bronze statues of the girls by local artist Linda Egle stand nearby. The people of Thedford will never forget.

Main and Walnut Streets, Thedford, 308-645-2489

TIP

Middle Loup River Ranch Guest House provides homestyle lodging for travelers exploring the Halsey-Thedford area.
402-430-6794

PERUSE NEW CREATIONS
AT OLD FEED STORE ART CENTER

The name creates its own artistic image: a former feed store in a small Sandhills town is transformed into an art gallery, right? No, the old feed store actually stands next door to this building, but it is a catchy name. Volunteers spent hundreds of hours renovating this structure, one of the oldest in town, into the modern gallery now showcasing local and regional art.

There are three galleries. The largest is dedicated to the current featured artist. This has included Russian-born painter Yelena Khanevskaya, painting Sandhills rancher Laron McGinn, National Geographic photographer Joel Sartore, and yours truly. I appreciate all the Sandhills scenes, real and imagined, that are displayed here. The center also hosts field trips and artist receptions. If you're coming from a long distance, I recommend calling first to make sure a volunteer is scheduled. Free admission.

104 Clark St., Bassett, 402-760-1058

TIP

A restored 1930s Phillips 66 gas station stands less than a block north of Old Feed Store Art Center.

SALUTE HISTORY
AT FORT HARTSUFF STATE HISTORICAL PARK

Tensions were high between settlers and Native Americans on the edge of the Sandhills in the 1870s. Fort Hartsuff was established to provide security and protect the allied Pawnee against their Sioux enemies. Soldiers stationed at Fort Hartsuff didn't see much action, but one skirmish stands out—the Battle of the Blowout.

On April 8, 1876, northwest of present-day Burwell near Jones Canyon, settlers, trappers, and a group of traveling prospectors chased a small band of natives across the landscape. Running for their lives, they were holed up in a blowout—an area of bare sand—when men from Fort Hartsuff arrived. Shots were exchanged and the siege continued past sunset. A sergeant was killed, and one native was severely wounded. The natives triumphantly escaped under the cover of darkness. Three Fort Hartsuff men were awarded the Congressional Medal of Honor for their actions. The era is relived with entertainment, games, and reenactors each year during the park's Spring Muster.

82034 Fort Ave., Burwell, 308-346-4715, outdoornebraska.gov/forthartsuff

TIP

While in the area, make sure to grab a burger at Elyria Bar in Elyria.
297 Valley Ave., 308-728-9924

DROP BY THE VILLAGE THAT NEVER EXISTED
AT HARROP SANDHILLS PARK

Organizers had big plans for Harrop. In the 1920s, streets were platted, lots sold, and a few buildings even went up. John Harrop, who had operated Harrop Post Office out of his rural home since 1912, moved to the new townsite imagined by his son, Omaha attorney Roy Harrop. A 1929 Nebraska Supreme Court ruling against a proposed irrigation project became a deathblow to the envisioned village. But in a way, Harrop lives on.

Harrop Sandhills Park is a convenient leg-stretching spot along a 60-mile stretch of asphalt between Taylor and Bassett. Native plants are marked along a short walking trail up scenic sand hills. The park allows camping and has an outhouse and a picnic shelter. A Nebraska Historical Marker tells the tale of how Harrop came to be, even though it really never did.

Harrop Sandhills Park is between Taylor and Rose on US Hwy.183, near mile marker 142.

TIP

Calamus Lodge offers lodging in its onsite motel and a spacious campground.

46358 828 Rd., Burwell, 308-346-4331

WITNESS

WORLD WAR I–ERA RUINS AT ANTIOCH

Ancient ruins catch the gaze of passersby traveling Nebraska Highway 2 in Sheridan County. Some call it Nebraska's Stonehenge, but we'll save that for another Sandhills attraction (#29). Near Antioch, concrete pillars and foundations, rusting steel, memories, and a few photos are about all that remain of Western Nebraska's once-booming potash industry. The plants built to extract potash from alkaline lakes popped up after the European potash supply was restricted during World War I. Antioch, Lakeside, and Hoffland grew overnight as hundreds of workers arrived to produce the potash used in fertilizer and other products.

After the war, cheaper European potash flooded the market, and Nebraska's potash industry dried up. So did the boomtowns—three residents live in Antioch today. The Knight Museum and Sandhills Center in Alliance (#61) dedicates a sizable exhibit to Nebraska's gone but not forgotten industrial contribution to World War I.

See ruins and a Nebraska Historical Marker dedicated to Nebraska's potash industry 1 mile west of Antioch on the north side of Nebraska Hwy. 2.

TIP

Historian Becky Herian is the undisputed expert when it comes to Nebraska's World War I potash era.

bherian@hotmail.com

STUFF YOURSELF
AT THE SENECA TURKEY DINNER & BAZAAR

Travelers craving home cooking and colorful culture will find both at the annual Turkey Dinner & Bazaar in Seneca. The event, hosted by United Church of Christ Fellowship, has been a tradition as long as resident LaVina Sevier can remember. Sevier was 92 when I attended in 2022.

Volunteers whip up 60 pounds of potatoes, three roasters of dressing, six gallons of corn, and eight 24-pound turkeys. Visitors bring side dishes and desserts. Pastor Les Parmenter quiets the room with prayer before asking, "Where do you want it?" while dishing out gravy. The crowd often swells to 300. Not bad for the unincorporated village of 45 people. The dinner raises funds to support the church. So does the silent auction, and merchandise like cutlery, dish towels, and bagged pecans. I'm there for horseradish. Seneca is known for the pungent root planted by families when the CB&Q Railroad founded the village in 1888. Residents dig it up and grind it. Don't dilly-dally: the 150 to 200 jars sell fast.

111 W Ave., Seneca, 308-639-3250

TALK STOCK
AT SANDHILLS HERITAGE MUSEUM

Want to get these museum volunteers worked up? Bawl about the desirable traits of Black Angus cattle as you moo-ve through this former bank turned museum. They have a thing for Herefords at Sandhills Heritage Museum in Dunning, those reddish and white cattle known for their ability—like Sandhillers—to survive harsh conditions. Hereford art fills display cases and walls. The Home State Bank vault door remains, and the collection includes vintage dresses, ornate post office boxes, cattle brands burned into wood, and other colorful history.

"Organizers thought building Dunning near where the Dismal and Middle Loup rivers meet would protect it from prairie fires, but Dunning has burned at least four times," said volunteer Vickie Webb. This museum is open weekends Memorial Day through Labor Day, or by appointment, and you can feel the volunteers' fiery passion for their history. That's no bull.

416 Jewett Ave., Dunning
308-880-0787 or 308-430-0786, facebook.com/sandhillsheritagemuseum

TIP

Hereford Crossroads is an annual reception for ranchers and others involved with the breed. In addition to a beef dinner, the event includes inductions into the Hereford Crossroads Hall of Fame.
308-430-0786

REFLECT
AT THE CATHEDRAL OF THE SANDHILLS

Anselmo's skyline is formed by the grain elevator and bins flanking Nebraska Highway 2. But if you peer through the trees south of the road, the ornate bell tower of St. Anselm's Catholic Church might catch your gaze. This house of worship is better known as the Cathedral of the Sandhills.

That bell tower stands 95 feet over the community, including the historic 1880s jail standing downtown. Stonecutters from Kansas created the church's limestone spires. Local men helped build it in the Late Gothic Revival style from 1927 to 1928. The original church, built in 1905, remains and is used as the parish hall. I stopped by early one Sunday morning as the arched windows glowed with the reflection of the first light of the day. The front doors are always open. A guestbook in the vestibule shows the names of travelers from far beyond the Sandhills.

201 W Rolla Ave., Anselmo, 308-749-2254, stjoescatholic.org

TIP

Chandler's Sandhill Honey offers natural and flavored honey, raw local honeycomb, and beeswax gifts from its roadside shop in Anselmo.
chandlersandhillhoney.com, 308-880-1733

77

PAY RESPECTS TO NEBRASKA'S STORY CATCHER

IN OLD JULES COUNTRY

Mari Sandoz died before I was born. So, I got acquainted through her books, and by exploring the basement archive of the Mari Sandoz High Plains Heritage Center at Chadron State College. And there were warm visits with her last surviving sibling, Caroline Sandoz Pifer (1910–2012), and their niece, Celia Sandoz Ostrander Barth, Mari's inspiration for *Winter Thunder*.

Mari's father, Jules Sandoz, once told her he considered writers and artists the maggots of society. From his deathbed decades later, he asked her to write his life story. She personified "starving artist" until *Old Jules* was published in 1935. The $5,000 nonfiction prize she received from *The Atlantic* is equal to $100,000 today. In novels like *The Beaver Men*, *Crazy Horse*, and *The Story Catcher*, Sandoz brought fur trappers, Native Americans, and pioneers to life. When her life ended, Sandoz was buried on a hillside overlooking her father's orchard. I sometimes read from the bench near her headstone.

From the Mari Sandoz Nebraska Historical Marker along Nebraska Hwy. 27 between Ellsworth and Gordon, travel 3.5 miles east on 365th Trail to reach Mari's grave. The ranch is home to Deer Meadows Outfitters.

78

RIDE THE WIND
INTO HYANNIS

Sandhills travelers will notice an abundance of windmills dotting the rolling landscape. As a critical part of the ranching industry—used for getting water to cattle—windmills are expected. What may be a surprise to travelers pulling into Hyannis is the windmill in the middle of Main Avenue. Each June, residents and visitors gather for Windmill Days with a car show, a pet parade, karaoke, a chuckwagon feed at All Saints Church, fishing tournament at Frey Lake, horseshoes at the Grant County Fairgrounds, an open-air church service at Centennial Park (up the street from the windmill), and more. The Grant County Museum will be open, too.

To me, the most surprising discovery I made at this museum, which is inside the Grant County Courthouse, is actor John Wayne's saddle from the movie *True Grit*. Turns out that Wayne's stuntman in the movie *Hondo* was actor Chuck Hayward of Hyannis. The saddle highlights Hayward's collection of Hollywood memorabilia on display in the museum.

facebook.com/hyanniswindmilldays

TIP

The Nebraska Sand Hills National Natural Landmark covers 28,872 acres on privately owned land south of Hyannis.

nps.gov

BID 'EM UP
AT BASSETT LIVESTOCK AUCTION

The sales arena at Bassett Livestock Auction has theater seats, but this is no movie house, and the guy on the horse isn't an actor. Years of experience gained during Wednesday sales has engrained in this pony when to back up, go forward, and get out of the way. But what does a weekly livestock sale have to do with travel? This, my friends, is a showcase of Sandhills culture. Visitors are welcome.

Trucks hauling trailers arrive and animals are unloaded into pens. Buyers head to the office to register before grabbing coffee in the café, where dessert is already baking. They settle into their favorite spots as Sandhills cattle move in. Barely discernible nods register as bids, so be careful if you need to scratch your nose! Sellers and buyers come and go as the cafe griddle sizzles with burgers—all beef, of course. I know from experience that the peach pie here is worth the visit.

105 W 4th St., Bassett, 402-684-2361, bassettlivestock.com

TIP

When leaving Bassett on US Hwy. 20 to the west, look north to see the late Dick Tracy's and his wife, Susan's, patriotic red, white, and blue barn. Please be safe when pulling over to view this Sandhills original.

SURPRISE YOUR SWEETHEART
WITH A VALENTINE FROM VALENTINE

Since 1941, the Valentine Post Office has offered a special Valentine's Day postmark in early February. Each year, thousands of Valentine's Day notes and cards are mailed to the Valentine Post Office to be placed in special "With Love from Valentine" envelopes and mailed to sweethearts around the world. The special Valentine's Day service truly is a labor of love.

Valentines being forwarded to Nebraska addresses need to reach the Valentine Post Office by February 10, and no later than February 8 for valentines being sent elsewhere within the United States. There is no extra charge for the special postmark. Valentines may also be sent via Priority Mail Express overnight service. Lovebirds wanting to have valentines postmarked in Valentine should address their envelopes, ensure appropriate first-class postage is affixed, put the envelope(s) inside a larger envelope (also with postage), and send or hand-deliver to:

Valentine's Day Postmark, Postmaster, 239 N Hall St., Valentine NE 69201

TIP

Sandhills travelers can learn about events, outdoor adventures, attractions, dining, lodging, seasonal fun, and more at sandhillswesternvacations.rocks.

TASTE THE WORLD'S BEST WATER IN AMELIA

In some areas of the Sandhills, subterranean water is under so much natural pressure that it gushes from the ground. A water fountain in Amelia has gurgled with a constant supply for decades. I stop to fill whatever bottles are rolling around in my car. I'm not the only one—the flow of visitors arriving with empty jugs is almost as constant as the well itself, with each carload often doubling Amelia's population. A sign claims six residents. Local rancher Kelly Cameron told me the population is now four.

Local legend recounts a 1950s history book attributing Amelia with the purest water on earth. I've never met anyone who remembered ever seeing the book, but that doesn't keep people from proudly claiming the water as 99.9 percent pure. Amelia has dried up since having more than 100 residents a century ago. It's named for former resident Amelia Bliss. How blissful it must be to have a constant supply of the world's best water . . . and no water bills.

11 miles northwest of Chambers on 856th Rd.

TIP

Another flowing well is available to the public at the Goose Lake 4-H Club's Dew Drop Inn Park southeast of O'Neill on 848th Rd.

MEET THE VILLAGERS
IN TAYLOR

Nobody saw me. I was driving through Taylor, noticed a man waving, and I waved back. I looked again and he was . . . black and white. They were all over town—not a speck of color on any of them. This was no zombie apocalypse. I had just met the Taylor Villagers.

Resident Marah Sandoz made her first life-size painted plywood silhouette in 2003 with hopes of getting travelers to slow down and stay a while. It worked. Visitors brake for Villager selfies or come to look for them all. There are 150 so far in Taylor and Loup County. Sandoz makes them in the backroom workshop at Marah's Treasures, right next door to Marah's Tea Room. Some are modeled after actual residents. Others are imagined visions of the past, like Ralph and Hank outside the former Farmers Filling Station that is now the Taylor Visitor Information Center. No villagers, real or otherwise, were harmed when an explosion left a downtown building in splinters in 2021. They didn't even flinch.

304 Broadway St., Taylor, 308-214-0847, taylorne.com/villagers

TIP

The conical trees at Taylor Park are not manicured, they are Taylor Junipers, a natural variant of the eastern red cedar tree that never needs trimming. The mutant was discovered here and is now sold by greenhouses nationwide.

taylorne.com

CLIMB INTO A BARN LOFT
ALONG THE SANDHILLS JOURNEY NATIONAL SCENIC BYWAY

Nebraska Highway 2 is known as the Sandhills Journey National Scenic Byway. The byway route begins in Grand Island and stretches through farmland and sand hills for 272 miles to Alliance. A two-story barn in Broken Bow serves as the byway's spacious visitor center. There's a new sod house out back.

The visitor center is open Memorial Day through Labor Day and contains a collection of more than 110 types of barbed wire and exhibits on the railroad, ranching, the Loup River system, and the Sandhills. A trail outside leads past prairie plants and a pond to a working windmill. The late CBS Television host Charles Kuralt once declared Nebraska Highway 2 as "one of America's 10 most beautiful highways." It might be a lofty statement, but as far as I'm concerned, the other nine don't have anything on the Sandhills Journey National Scenic Byway.

44106 NE Hwy. 2, Broken Bow, 308-872-8331, sandhillsjourney.com

TIP

When passing through Broken Bow toward Sandhills adventures, I almost always stop at Prairie Grounds Cafe & Gifts.

308-872-3333, facebook.com/prairiegroundscoffeehouse

AVOID THE CLARINET
AT CENTENNIAL HALL MUSEUM

This brick structure with rows of arched windows has been a Valentine landmark since 1897. Claim to fame: It's the oldest standing high school building in Nebraska. Pioneer belongings, religious artifacts, and local school and military relics fill the former classrooms. A visitor will occasionally ring one of the 1,700 bells in the museum's Hallock Bell Collection. Some say that's not the only music heard here. Even though the instruments were removed decades ago, visitors report notes coming from the school's former music room.

Local folklore recounts the death of a female student in the 1940s after her clarinet reed was poisoned. Is her disembodied presence responsible for the ghostly tunes or the rocking chair seen rocking on its own? Probably not. My friends over at the Cherry County Historical Society have been unable to authenticate that the murder ever took place. Spiritual energy aside, there's something else unexpected lurking here, a thrift shop.

3rd and Macomb Streets, Valentine, 402-376-1455

TIP

There's another museum in Valentine. A whiskey still, a large collection of spittoons, and a pair of weird weavings made from human hair are among the many quality curiosities preserved at the Cherry County Historical Society Museum.

249 S Main St., Valentine

402-376-2015

SPEND THE NIGHT IN A SHED AT SCHNEIDEREIT RANCH

Hotels are few in the Sandhills near Brewster. You could pitch a tent at Willow Lake or spend the night in Ivan and Amy Schneidereit's shed. "The Shed" is a steel building with enough amenities for a comfortable stay. Don't mind the bear and giraffe out front. Ivan's dad, Carl, made them.

The story goes that as a young girl, Ivan's mom, Roberta, "Birdy," dreamt she'd marry a man who had a pet giraffe. After marrying, her husband made her one, using Sandhills sand to make the cement. And the bear? Well, times were lean. Carl's real pet bear was sacrificed for the wedding reception meal. The bear sculpture memorializes the animal. Guests go birding, fishing, canoeing, and stargazing, or help with cattle branding, milking cows and goats, and gathering eggs. Ivan's ancestors founded the ranch in 1885. Please call before visiting.

42534 German Valley Rd., Brewster, 308-547-2257

MORE BREWSTER LODGING

Sandhills Guest Ranch Bed & Breakfast
42852 W North Loup Rd., 308-547-2460

Uncle Buck's Lodge
455 Brewster Ave., 308-547-2210, unclebuckslodge.com

LEARN SANDHILLS HISTORY
AT LAKELAND SOD HIGH SCHOOL

When the Great Depression prevented families in southwest Brown County from sending their children to town for education, they built their own school out of prairie sod. The school operated from 1934 until better economic times in 1941. Locals believe it was the only sod building in US history ever built specifically as a high school. A marker dedicated to Lakeland Sod High School is located near Long Lake, which until recently was home to my favorite place in the Sandhills, a neglected but serene State Recreation Area. Grass can obscure the marker, now bearing the rusty high-water mark from floods in 2019.

The Lakeland Sod High School marker is northeast of Elsmere, 5.5 miles north of the junction of Moon Lake Ave. and Elsmere Rd. A Nebraska Historical Marker dedicated to the school stands west of Ainsworth along US Hwy. 20.

TIP

Willow Lake Wildlife Management Area is 4 miles south of Long Lake. Amenities are limited to a boat dock, an outhouse, and a small camping area, but the lake is home to largemouth bass, bluegill, and yellow perch; and flocks of ducks, geese, cormorants, pelicans, and other migratory Sandhills residents.

Joe McBride shaping a hat
at Ranch-Land Western Store in Ainsworth.

SHOPPING AND FASHION

TRADE UP
AT FORT CODY TRADING POST

North Platte was once the last bastion of civilization for travelers headed west. Native American and pioneer trails paralleled the Platte River, and cavalrymen patrolled the region to keep the peace. Nowadays, Interstate 80 motorists speed by at 75 miles per hour, but they should brake for this world-class attraction resembling a frontier fort. Travelers leaving Interstate 80 at exit 177 are greeted by a 40-foot-tall silhouette of Buffalo Bill. Being equal parts bookstore, souvenir shop, jewelry store, museum, and amusement park makes this Nebraska's coolest roadside curiosity.

Nowhere else can you get a new coonskin cap, see a two-headed taxidermy calf, and watch a hand-carved, 20,000-piece, motorized Buffalo Bill's Wild West Show churn to life every 20 minutes. Out in the stockade, one of the few remaining 1960s Muffler Men statues is adorned like a Native American standing watch over the wagons, jail, and the Fort Cody Music Series.

221 Halligan Dr., North Platte, 308-532-8081, fortcody.com

TIP

The 20th Century Veterans Memorial pays tribute to Americans who served in our country's military, and the volunteers of North Platte's famous World War II Canteen. Visitors can also see the Lincoln County Law Enforcement Memorial.

visitnorthplatte.com

SCORE SOME ZZZS
AT SANDHILLS SUITES

This historic structure, standing on Burwell's vibrant town square, began life back in 1908 as a 25-room hotel. After later serving as apartments for decades, the building's current owner renovated the place into the unique luxury lodging destination that Sandhills Suites is today. Each room has original hardwood flooring, along with a big-screen TV, queen-size bed, pull-out couch, Wi-Fi, kitchenette, and street parking, all of which are enjoyed by overnight visitors headed to Calamus Reservoir (#45), Nebraska's Big Rodeo (#53), or Fort Hartsuff State Historical Park (#71).

The Hub (#91) is across the street from Sandhills Suites. The Spot is a diner just off the east side of the square, and the Double Yolk Cafe is around the corner. Find more Burwell businesses and attractions elsewhere in this guide. Sandhills Suites is a convenient and restful launch point for Sandhills adventures.

412 Grand Ave., Burwell, 308-346-4964, sandhillssuites.com

TIP

A stay at Sandhills Suites includes locally brewed coffee from Normal Roasting Company, which has its roastery and coffee shop across the square. My favorite is their Sandhills Blend. Normal's coffee subscriptions keep Sandhills memories warm, no matter where you call home.

308-346-4655, normalroastingcompany.com

HUM CAROLS ALL YEAR LONG
AT SOMETHING SPECIAL BY MARILYN

Christmas comes but once a year, but at Something Special By Marilyn it's Christmas every day. Christmas ornament collectors discover more than 5,000 kinds here, and an estimated 10,000 holiday and gift items. The store, founded by Marilyn Gokie and her daughter, Janell Rossman, began in 1994 with a small selection of holiday offerings in the corner of a downtown building. When Gokie went on vacation, her daughter expanded the selection. The next time she vacationed, it happened again. Something Special By Marilyn grew to be the largest holiday-themed gift store in Nebraska. Customers sipping hot cider stroll up and down the spiral staircase to showrooms on four levels.

Marilyn Gokie died in 2018. Her love of holiday décor lives on here and in the homes and businesses of thousands of customers. Happy holidays!

204 S Main St., Atkinson, 402-925-2754, somethingspecialbymarilyn.com

TIP

The staff at Marilyn's suggests Atkinson visitors book rooms at Sandhills Guest House Motel and spend the weekend shopping!
402-925-5600, atkinsonmotel.com

TRY ON BOOTS AND SPURS
AT MORGAN'S COWPOKE HAVEN

Few businesses can claim a heritage stretching to the Wild West. The only store in Ellsworth can. Morgan's Cowpoke Haven began as the Spade Ranch Store in 1898. The Spade Ranch, which once spanned more than 500,000 acres, is still in operation. Before she became a successful writer, young Mari Sandoz would come to the store with her father, Old Jules (#77). The stories overheard between homesteaders and cowboys influenced her writing, decades later.

Sandoz's books sell well at Morgan's, and the store still outfits Spade Ranch cowboys, workers from other ranches, and travelers with clothing and tack. The floor creaks like an old wood floor should and that's how owner Wade Morgan likes it. He runs the place with his longtime partner, JoLynn McKinney. I suggest asking for one of her homemade sandwiches before perusing the largest selection of sporting goods available for miles. They sell tons of guns here. After all, this is still the Wild West.

1358 NE Hwy. 27, Ellsworth, 308-762-2666

TIP

Nebraska Hwy. 27 between Ellsworth and Gordon is known as the Mari Sandoz Sandhills Trail.

ROLL
INTO THE HUB

When H. J. "Pard" Coffin opened his three-story building in Burwell in the early 1900s, he wanted it to be the hub of commerce for a 60-mile radius. There were dentists' and doctors' offices, Burwell's first library and first telephone company, and an Odd Fellows Hall. Coffin's great-great grandson, John Schere, told me, "It was the Walmart of its day." After growing up in Burwell and leaving for decades, Schere moved home in 2006 and bought his great-great-grandfather's building. After undertaking repairs and renovations, Schere and his wife, Melissa, opened The Hub.

Shakes and other ice cream treats flow from the 1953 Bastian-Blessing soda fountain. The Scheres also whip up baked goods, smoothies, teas, and coffee drinks, and Polish dogs, hot dogs, and other lunchtime goodies. Local products fill shelves. Last time I was there, visitors were perusing antiques, residents were sipping morning coffee, and girls from the Burwell Longhorns volleyball team were having a Bible study. Truly the hub of the community.

180 Grand Ave., Burwell, 308-346-4674, facebook.com/thehubburwellne

TIP

A brick marker commemorating the 1872 homestead of Charles H. Jones, the first homesteader in Garfield County, stands northwest of Burwell on Jones Canyon Rd.

MORE BURWELL SHOPPING DESTINATIONS

Holy Heifer & Co.
Graphic T-shirts, shoes, jeans, and accessories.
180 Grand Ave., 308-219-0408
holyheiferco.com

Hello Lovely Boutique
Nebraska Cornhuskers items, business casual clothing, and bath items.
412 Grand Ave., 308-258-1546
hellolovelyboutique-ne.com

Dry Creek Western Wear
Cowboy boots, hats, Western shirts, workwear, jewelry, accessories, clothing for men, women, and children.
827 G St., 308-346-4810
drycreekwesternwear.com

INDULGE IN FABULOUS AND FUNKY AT SANDHILLS SAGE

Johnstown, population 63, is usually quiet. Exceptions are during the Brown County Fair each Labor Day weekend, when the L Bow Room Bar (#6) has karaoke, and four times a year when Sandhills Sage opens its doors to shoppers. The seasonal shopping experience happens two weekends in the spring, two weekends in the summer, two weekends in the fall, and well, you get it. Pam Theis, who owns the business with partners Jennifer Martin and Hayley Williams, said that the limited hours increase demand, and gives the trendy trio time to upcycle, reupholster, paint, and otherwise prepare their ever-changing inventory.

Last time I was there, pumpkin-scented candles seemed to put buyers in the mood. They were stocking up on T-shirts, lamps, baskets, quilted throws, vases, books, pillows, framed art, antlers, and painted four-pane windows. Fans of the CBS TV movie *O Pioneers!*, adapted from the novel of the same name by Nebraskan Willa Cather, may recognize Sandhills Sage's building in some scenes.

307 Main St., Johnstown, 402-322-0380

93

PICK A PECK
OF PICKLED PLEASURE AT THE PEA PATCH

A car sticking from the ground Carhenge style (#29), a rusty truck, and an American flag windsock announce The Pea Patch to passersby on Nebraska Highway 91, west of Burwell. When I finally stopped after passing by for years, manager Missy Sedlacek was shooing peacocks from the greenhouse. More than 1,000 varieties of annuals and perennials fill the racks, but The Pea Patch isn't only open during spring and summer.

The gift shop is busy all year long with people shopping for jelly, salsa, seven varieties of dill pickles, pickled jalapeno slices, whole peppers, okra, and so much more. Sedlacek and her mother—business owner Terese Lech—fill more than 5,000 jars each year! They plant 300 hills of cucumbers in preparation for pickle making. In September, they set out glassware, vintage toys, rusty tools, yard art, and peacock tailfeathers for Nebraska's Junk Jaunt (#100). Regular Pea Patch customers return their jars.

46143 NE Hwy. 91, Burwell, 308-346-5040, facebook.com/peapatchgreenhouse

TIP

Free ice water at the Taylor Visitor Information Center is reason enough to pull over. Inside, brochures fill racks so weary travelers can cool off and plan their next stop.

Intersection of Hwys. 91 and 183, Taylor

SHAPE UP
AT RANCH-LAND WESTERN STORE

Joe McBride was 12 when he learned to shape cowboy hats. All these years later, after a cowboy or cowgirl's hat gets bent during a buck off or other incident, McBride fires up his steamer and massages out the dents. His reputation draws customers from hundreds of miles away to his Ranch-Land Western Store. The downtown Ainsworth building began in 1914 as a hardware store and has also served as a mortuary. McBride's parents, Mort and Louise, moved their western store here in 1963. Joe bought his parents out in 1988.

Ranch-Land sells cowboy hats and boots, jeans, shirts, and outerwear—including bison-, goat-, elk-, and deer-skin gloves. The inventory includes boutique items for women. Ranch-Land also crafts leather purses, belts, and tack, and if you need a replacement conch on your saddle, they can take care of that, too. Unexpected is the American-made cutlery for sale. A memorial hat tree near the ceiling displays the headgear of area ranchers who have trotted on to greener Sandhills pastures.

209 N Main St., Ainsworth, 402-387-2724, ranchlandwestern.com

TIP

The Sellors-Barton Museum is in a log structure, and the Coleman House and Brown County Historical Society's Dixon House are repositories of local history and genealogy. All are on the north side of US Hwy. 20 in Ainsworth.

BRING LIFE
TO THE GHOST TOWN OF WOOD LAKE

Fifty-one people live in Wood Lake. Lifelong resident Jean Pinney knows them all and objected to me characterizing her community as a ghost town. Her friend, Norma Cozad, opened Grandma's Playhouse and Ice Cream Shoppe in 2005 to add a little life to the community—500 people lived here a century ago.

Cozad sells ice cream, cold drinks, and baked goods, and heats things up with her cranberry jalapeno and other spicy jellies. She opens early for morning coffee. Last time I visited was the last Saturday in July. I walked out with a jar of sand cherry jelly and an invite to the annual Wood Lake Volunteer Fire Department Barbecue. A local rancher donates the meat. Firefighters cook it while shoppers peruse the craft show. People show up at Wood Lake Village Park with sides, salads, and desserts, and everyone digs in as the village's population swells five-fold. The street dance begins at sunset. Wood Lake is not a ghost town—it has plenty of spirit.

108 E US Hwy. 20, Wood Lake, 402-322-1940

TIP

South of Valentine, Brownlee Rd. leads through one of my favorite stretches of scenic Sandhills. Passing through the unincorporated community of Brownlee, the road eventually links with Nebraska Hwy. 97.

96

BOOK IT
TO PLAINS TRADING COMPANY BOOKSELLERS

Bookstores are few and far between, and this one is among the nation's best. I first stopped here more than two decades ago for *The Last Prairie: A Sandhills Journal*. I've been buying books here ever since. Duane Gudgel, who co-owns the store with his wife, Darlene Meyer, is a kindred spirit when it comes to appreciation for the Sandhills. In addition to books in just about every genre, he stocks the largest selection about the natural history of the Sandhills and Great Plains that I've seen anywhere. They also carry the latest releases for people who enjoy reading about cowboys and settlers, the contemporary West, and Native American topics—including the local Lakota and Sioux Nation.

Plains Trading Company also carries Nebraska wine, toys, works by areas artists—including Gudgel's photography—and a variety of high-quality souvenir and gift items for Sandhills travelers.

269 N Main St., Valentine, 402-376-1424, plainstrading.com

TIP

Young's Western Wear offers visitors 20,000 square feet of saddles, boots, hats, and other cowboy duds.

143 N Main St., Valentine, 402-376-1281

HAVE YOUR NOGGIN MEASURED
AT BAR NONE HAT COMPANY

Kaycee Orr-Hoffman is no mad hatter. From her shop in Thedford, this ranch wife, mom, and businesswoman makes high-end hats for cowboys, cowgirls, and others needing a cover over their dome. She comes from a long line of well-known female hatters. The "bar none," a straight line with an open circle beneath it, was branded onto thousands of her family's Herefords over many generations. Now, that brand appears on the lining of her hats. Orr-Hoffman's shop along Nebraska Highway 2 is equipped with machines that aren't made anymore. She measured my head with a French Conformateur made in the 1800s. It creates patterns for making hats just the right shape and size.

Orr-Hoffman's suggested hat etiquette includes always removing your hat when entering a building, taking your hat off at the dinner table, never laying your hat on a bed—it's bad luck, and always tipping your hat to a lady. 'Nuff said.

39313 NE Hwy. 2, Thedford, 970-590-5151, barnonehats.com

TIP

My friends at the Upper Loup Natural Resources District take care of a beautiful arboretum planted near the Thedford Rural Fire Hall.
39252 NE Hwy. 2, Thedford, 308-645-2250

HAPPEN UPON
THE MOST UNLIKELY PLACE

A Sandhills village of 230 residents might seem like an unlikely place to find one of Nebraska's premier art galleries. Even more unlikely is that this is also a cafe with brunch, lunch, specialty coffees, chai tea, wine, and beer. This is The Most Unlikely Place. Locals and regulars call it The MUP. Siblings Dennis Miller, Rex MIller, and Jean Jensen own the place along with Dennis's wife, Cynthia. Jean is known for her paintings of flora and fauna. Dennis prefers painting Western Nebraska scenes. Rex is known for his wood, brass, marble, and etched glass sculptures. Guest artists are also featured, and The MUP schedules regular live music performances and speakers.

When sandhill cranes descend on the North Platte River each spring (#59), The MUP becomes HQ for visiting birders. The MUP sells local products, gift items, and a variety of books by Nebraska authors and others. Finding such diverse offerings elsewhere in the Sandhills is most unlikely.

205 Main St., Lewellen, 308-778-9557, themostunlikelyplace.com

TIP

Crescent Lake National Wildlife Refuge, Clear Creek Wildlife Management Area, and Garden County Wildlife Refuge all are near Lewellen and offer opportunities for wildlife viewing.
visitgardencounty.com

CHECK OUT
SECOND CHAPTER BREWING

Richard Gibson and Lisa Kraus opened a new chapter for Ogallala when they bought the community's former Goodall City Library and opened their brewery in 2023. Some people still come by hoping to drop off borrowed books (Ogallala's new library is down the street). Now when people visit the brewery created with a library theme—books fill shelves and tasting flight boards resemble card catalog drawers—they leave with bestsellers, none of which ever have to be returned!

Four- and six-packs of beers like Oga-Lager, Witty Librarian, and Czeched Out fill the "to-go fridge." And just like a good book, it's hard to put down the Trashy Romance Seltzer. T-shirts, hats, beanies, and hoodies are among the souvenir and gift items for sale. Ogallala's craft beer fans and visiting aficionados speak volumes when they say Second Chapter Brewing was long overdue.

203 W A St., Ogallala, 308-284-7391, secondchapterbrewing.com

TIP

The Bunkhouse is a rustic bar and grill known for its Chicken Bacon Ranch Pizza and much more. Look up to see the tanned animal skins and other curiosities tacked to the ceiling. Located catty-corner from Arthur Village Park.

306 Fir St., Arthur, 308-764-2601

FILL YOUR TRUNK
DURING NEBRASKA'S JUNK JAUNT

What's better than a garage sale? How about hundreds of vendors in dozens of communities along nearly 500 miles of deals and discovery, twisting through the Sandhills. Scavenging their closets, basements, attics, sheds, and barns for rusty gold, nearly 500 registered vendors set up for the epic bargain bonanza known as Nebraska's Junk Jaunt. Thousands of shoppers, affectionately known as "Junkers," come for the thrill of the hunt.

The event's official shopper guide lists what vendors have for sale. Friends, families, and collectors use it to strategize—often before dawn in small-town cafes and coffee shops. Many split up to better cover the Junk Jaunt route. Food vendors along the way keep the treasure hunters fueled up. Elba, on the Loup Rivers Scenic Byway (#43), is known for the Junk Jaunt enchiladas sold as a community fundraiser, and for Charlie's Station that sells hundreds of dozens of homemade kolaches during the three-day event. You'll leave Junk Jaunt with junk in your trunk and your belly full, too.

308-346-5151, junkjaunt.com

TIP

Communities along the Junk Jaunt route are not accustomed to traffic jams and lack of parking, and out-of-towners excited about bargain hunting often brake suddenly. Stay safe out there!

ACTIVITIES
BY SEASON

SPRING

SUMMER

FALL

WINTER

SUGGESTED
ITINERARIES

CULTURAL GEMS

BACK TO NATURE

ONLY IN THE SANDHILLS

HEARTLAND HISTORY

COWBOY CUISINE

TOAST THE SANDHILLS

FRIENDS AND FAMILY

MAKE A SPLASH

BEST OF THE BYWAYS

SMALL TOWN STOPS

INDEX

NEBRASKAland Days parade in North Platte.